Neighbour Disputes:
Responses by
Social Landlords

by **Valerie Karn**
Rachel Lickiss
John Crawley
and **David Hughes**

Institute of Housing

The Institute of Housing

The Institute of Housing is the professional organisation for people who work in housing. Its purpose is to take a strategic and leading role in encouraging and promoting the provision of good quality affordable housing for all. The Institute has more than 11,000 members working in local authorities, housing associations, the private sector and educational institutions.

Institute of Housing
Octavia House
Westwood Way
Coventry CV4 8JP
Telephone: 0203 694433

Published by the Institute of Housing

Neighbour Disputes: Responses by Local Authorities and Housing Associations

Authors: Valerie Karn, Rachel Lickiss, John Crawley and David Hughes
Editor: John Perry
© Institute of Housing 1993

ISBN 0 901607 68 1

Graphic design by Henry's House Design Co–operative Ltd.
Cover drawing by Marta Perez Muñoz
Illustration p.22–23 by Malcolm Willett
Printed by ?   .

Contents

iii

List Of Figures

About The Authors

Valerie Karn is Professor of Environmental Health and Housing at the University of Salford.

Rachel Lickiss is a Research Assistant at the University of Salford, Department of Environmental Health and Housing.

John Crawley is Director of Conflict Management Plus, a Consultancy on Mediation and Dispute Resolution.

David Hughes is a Senior Lecturer in the Faculty of Law at Leicester University.

Acknowledgements

The Authors wish to thank the ESRC for their financial support for the research on which this book is based and the Institute of Housing for funding its publication; the organisations and tenants who took the trouble to provide information for the study, and all those who have provided advice, encouragement and comments on the draft publication, notably David Leabeater of the National Consumer Council, Jim Wintour of the London Borough of Southwark, Jim McLaughlan of the City of Glasgow, Joyce Dobbin and Jo Garvey of the Northern Ireland Housing Executive, John Roe of the University of Salford and John Perry of the Institute of Housing. They would also like to thank TPAS (Scotland) and Paul Brown of the Legal Services Agency for permission to use the material in Appendix 3.

Information Sources

The material presented in this book is largely based on research carried out by a team from Salford and Leicester Universities into the role and effectiveness of tenants' complaints procedures in housing associations and local authorities. This project was part of the ESRC Citizen's Grievance Initiative.

The largest part of the study was devoted to conducting surveys of tenants' attitudes to complaining and actual complaining behaviour; 1,981 replies were received to a postal survey of 5,340 tenants of local authorities and housing associations (a 37.1 per cent response rate). From these respondents a non–random sample of tenants was selected to give a range of experiences of and reactions to dissatisfaction. A total of 144 in–depth interviews were conducted with these tenants to obtain data about causes of dissatisfaction, modes of complaint, knowledge of how to complain and the details of particular cases. In addition information was collected through case studies of nine social landlords, through national postal surveys of housing associations and local authority housing departments, and through individual exchanges with particular organisations. The findings of this research project were the basis of a report published by the National Consumer Council (1991) *Housing Complaints Procedures: Principles of Good Practice for Social Landlords*. Additional material on mediation in neighbour disputes has been collected subsequently in collaboration with John Crawley. Use is also made of a number of other studies listed in the references.

Preface

Disputes between neighbours are one of the most problematic and time–consuming areas of activity for housing associations, and even more so, for local authorities in their variety of roles, as landlord, implementor of environmental health legislation and as social services authority.

'For a housing manager, out of all ... managerial tasks, the solution of complaints about neighbour nuisance is the most difficult, time–consuming and inconclusive. Firstly, there is its lack of definition, the difficulty in quantifying the trivial and the serious. Secondly, there is the aggravation and entrenchment nuisance can cause between neighbours and the demands this makes on the manager's persuasive skills. Intervention should be impartial, but is fraught with pressure from either party to defend their point of view' (Grant, 1987, p.1).

There are no perfect or instant solutions to the dilemmas posed by neighbour disputes but there is a growing body of knowledge and experience of various types of approach. This book attempts to draw together that knowledge and experience.

In its *Housing Management Standards Manual* (IOH, 1993), the Institute of Housing gives considerable prominence to guidance on estate management standards for dealing with neighbour and nuisance problems. Here we amplify that guidance and examine in detail the ways in which local authorities and housing associations can and do deal with neighbour disputes. Currently the picture is one of much time–consuming involvement with the trivial but a tendency to back off from serious problems and leave people to sort out their own differences. When landlords do grapple with the problems, they tend to swing between attempts to persuade neighbours to act more considerately and threats of legal action, which in reality they are often reluctant to take. A more constructive approach to providing a long term solution, which is applicable in many cases, is mediation. This technique enables both sides of a dispute to assess and come to terms with their situation, before formulating and agreeing on a solution they can live with. The use and applicability of mediation in the resolution of neighbour disputes is discussed in detail including guidance on the practicalities of adopting such an approach.

But in some situations mediation is inappropriate or is unsuccessful. We therefore go on to discuss the various legal powers available to housing organisations and their applicability to different types of dispute.

It should be noted that although there is considerable common ground between some strategies for dealing with racial and sexual harassment and those for tackling other types of neighbour dispute, this book is not intended to be a guide to dealing with such harassment. (References on these subjects are included in the Bibliography.)

Chapter 1
Introduction: The Nature Of Neighbour Disputes And The Role Of Landlords

Neighbour disputes and the ways in which they can be tackled are inseparable from the wider issue of 'nuisance', which appears to be a matter of growing concern. For instance:

- In 1948, only about 23 per cent of people claimed to have been disturbed by external noise sources at home, whereas by 1961 the figure had risen to 50 per cent (Wilson, 1963).

- In 1985/86, 1,270 per million of the population reported domestic noise nuisance to environmental health officers (Hughes, 1992). In 1989, the figure had risen to 1,855 per million and in 1990/91, to 2,264 per million (IEHO 1992). This number was far in excess of complaints about noise from road traffic or industrial or commercial noise.

1.1 The Nature Of Neighbour Disputes

The commonest causes of complaints to environmental health officers about noise are amplified music and dogs (Hughes, 1992). Mediation agencies also find that noise is the most common cause of the neighbour disputes they deal with. The types of noise are wide–ranging, including for instance, besides amplified music, general domestic noise, DIY activity, television and radio, late night parties, barking dogs, musical instruments and revving engines.

But there are many types of environmental problem other than noise which affect people's 'quiet enjoyment' of their homes. In an interview survey of local authority and housing association tenants carried out by Salford University in 1989, the most common causes of neighbour disputes, apart from noise were:

- nuisance from pets, particularly dogs, vandalism and litter (Figure 1). Other problems were harassment, parking, drinking and drug–taking, car repairs in the street and racial disputes.

- in some areas bonfires are also a common source of disputes.

Growing public concern about these issues can be ascribed to a number of factors:

- high density housing environments, which combine badly with a rising dog population, owned and stray;

- inadequate levels of sound insulation in flats and terraced and semi–detached houses, combined with modern sound systems;

- the growing numbers of both young and elderly households living independently, but in close proximity, who find each others' lifestyles irksome.

The study by Salford University (see p.1) found that:

25 per cent of grievances concerned the behaviour of neighbours and 75 per cent of the tenants with these grievances complained to their landlord or some other agency. This figure has to be regarded as a minimum since not all cases are easily classifiable in this way. Complaints about specific neighbours inter–relate closely with general dissatisfaction about the local environment and may be expressed in that more general way. The distinction between these categories in the Salford study is therefore somewhat arbitrary depending on the way in which people described their complaint.

Figure 1 Types of Nuisance Caused by Neighbours

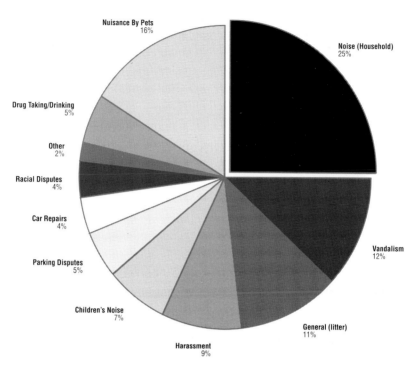

Source : Salford University Interview Survey of Tenants
(Figures relate to the main cause of nuisance for each grievance expressed as
a percentage of all grievances caused by neighbours, n=56)

Of course, the fact that people are bothered by noise, dogs, graffiti etc, does
not necessarily mean that they will complain either to neighbours about the
problem or about those neighbours to their landlord, the police or an
environmental health officer. Nevertheless, complaints about neighbours
represent a large proportion of all the complaints that landlords receive.

A study of complaints to local authorities found that grievances which
were not stated by the complainant as being against neighbours may in
fact have had this cause. For example, in the case of a family with four
grievances, three turned out to be linked to problems with neighbours.
Their complaint about housing allocation related to their desire to
move away from the noise, abuse and threats of their neighbours.

Their complaint about the standard of refuse collection arose from the behaviour of neighbours. A third complaint about the lack of children's play areas was caused by older children who bullied their younger children when they used local facilities (Simpson and McCarthy, 1990).

Most friction between neighbours probably remains at the level of irritation and never comes to the attention of landlords. But much escalates and in the most extreme cases, of deliberate damage, physical attacks, drunken behaviour and drug abuse, can take on a violent aspect.

1.2 The Role Of Local Authority And Housing Association Landlords In Dealing With Neighbour Disputes

The corollary of growing public concern about noise and other 'nuisance' has been growing pressure from the public for central and local government, and in particular social landlords, to act.

The central government response to nuisance has been piecemeal and mostly concerns noise, with some concern about dogs (DOE, 1990a, 1991 and 1992a).

• The DOE has introduced a package of enhanced planning guidance to reduce noise at source.

• Amended building regulations have been issued to provide enhanced noise insulation standards for flat conversions.

• As a result of a recommendation by the Noise Review Working Party (1990b), the Department of the Environment and the Home Office have produced a Joint Guidance Note on Control of Noisy Parties, summarising the existing powers of local authorities and the police (DOE, 1992c).

• A consultation paper on strengthening the legislation relating to noise was issued in June 1992, with a view to controlling street noise and loud speakers, and to seek views on the compulsory fitting of cut–out devices to burglar alarms (DOE 1992b). (Burglar alarms are currently governed

4

by a Code of Practice which is widely ignored, limiting the duration of the alarm to twenty minutes).

But much of the time, central government relies upon voluntary reductions of noise by those carrying out noisy activities (DOE, 1991) or failing that local authority action.

Inevitably it is to local, not central, government that the public normally turns in cases of nuisance. In particular, there is pressure from tenants of local authorities and housing associations (or their neighbours) for landlords to enforce conventional standards of behaviour on their tenants. There is frequently an expectation from the public that to achieve this the landlord has ready recourse to legal powers and remedies. This expectation is not usually fulfilled and grievances against neighbours are often translated into grievances against the landlord if they do not or cannot find a solution. This sense of grievance against the landlord is often based on unreal expectations of what the powers of the landlord are.

'... there is a clear expectation that they [the council] will not only enforce regulations and byelaws but also perform a disciplinary and adjudicatory function' (Simpson and McCarthy, 1990, p.26).

But in reality,

'... officers, members and tenants found it difficult to express precisely what the council – as landlord – should ideally be doing, even assuming it had the resources and the wherewithal to achieve it' (Keenan, 1992).

Neighbour disputes are particularly difficult for the law to deal with for a number of reasons:

• Legal action itself will only be available in a limited range of circumstances, for example,

> where the matter complained of amounts to the **civil wrong of nuisance**;

where it is actionable as a **criminal wrong** because it is a **statutory nuisance** within the meaning of the Environmental Protection Act 1990;

or where it amounts to a **breach of some other legal obligation**, for example a term in a **tenancy agreement** or **restrictive covenant**.

- In the public rented sector, even if landlords want to enforce certain standards of behaviour, their powers to do so have been severely eroded by the 1980 Housing Act (see now the Housing Act 1985), which gives tenants greater security of tenure (a move which is clearly desirable from many other points of view). By making it more difficult for public sector landlords to evict tenants, the Act has weakened the traditional sanction which landlords have held over their tenants. Although it should not be supposed that authorities behaved in a cavalier fashion towards their tenants before 1980 by dispossessing them regularly on managerial grounds, they were certainly able to deal with severe cases more easily. (Private sector landlords were already subject to restrictions under the Rent Act 1977, and continue to be so under the Housing Act 1988, legislation which also affects Housing Associations).

- The situation has also been exacerbated by the Right to Buy. Although landlords' control over tenants' behaviour has been weakened, it is still greater than that which a local authority or neighbours can exercise over home owners. As the recent case in Newham demonstrated, landlords are all too aware that by exercising the Right to Buy tenants can escape from enforcement of clauses in tenancy agreements, for instance, as in the Newham case, those relating to racial harassment (*Inside Housing* Vol 10, No 5, 5 Feb 1993 p.1). Some are using covenants on Right to Buy sales to try to create equality of treatment of owners and renters (See Legal Appendix 1.3).

- In many neighbour disputes the rights and wrongs of a situation are very unclear. And even in cases when the original source of dispute shows a clear innocent and guilty party, subsequent escalation of the dispute often tends to draw both sides into culpable behaviour.

- Where friction arises between two neighbouring occupiers, and one resorts to legal action and obtains a remedy, there will be the continuing problem of the successful party having to live near to a person s/he has successfully taken to law. It is not a recipe for harmony. For this reason alone, it may be supposed that legal action, whatever form it may take, will normally occur only when a situation is perceived by the initiator of the action as otherwise intolerable, though the perception of what is intolerable will vary from person to person, group to group and also according to the general level of litigiousness in society.

Thus, legal action does not provide an ideal long term solution to most neighbour disputes and seldom provides a short–term one either.

Because of these problems, there is some support, especially from within housing organisations for the view that landlords should not get involved in neighbour disputes because tenants should not be treated any differently from owners. However, there are compelling arguments for social landlords to get actively involved if necessary, in cases of extreme and incorrigible behaviour, by using legal measures, but more particularly to resolve disputes before they escalate.

In particular, social landlords have to take greater responsibility for relationships between their tenants (and between their tenants and other neighbours) because:

- Neighbour disputes are an important factor in determining whether an estate is a good living environment or not. Owners can ultimately vote with their feet; tenants cannot do so as readily. Landlords have a stake in the atmosphere of the estate since it directly affects their performance – turnover, voids, arrears levels, etc.

- There are increasing numbers of vulnerable people housed by these landlords. They include the poorest and most deprived households, single parents, the elderly, small children, ethnic minorities, homeless people and those discharged into the community under Community Care policies. They are both more likely to be complained about by neighbours and less able to resolve problems for themselves.

- Vulnerable groups, who are frequently the subject of complaints, need to be able to state their side of the story and have access to justice and support.

- There is a much greater tenure mix than in the past, arising from council house sales and scattered housing association purchases and construction, and so action in neighbour disputes has to be able to cross tenure boundaries rather than just involving landlord powers. Techniques such as mediation, which are discussed in detail in Chapters 5 and 6, can be used equally well to deal with disputes between tenants, owners, or between a tenant and neighbouring owner.

Dealing with neighbour disputes should be regarded as part of an overall policy for effective and efficient housing management and as part of a commitment to providing equal opportunities to members of the population who may be disadvantaged or discriminated against. This is especially true in the light of recent movements towards the adoption of Customer Care policies.

Chapter 2
Complaining Behaviour

The fundamental difficulty in dealing with neighbour complaints arises from the fact that they involve tenants with opposing points of view; there is frequently no clear picture of which one is 'sinned against' and which 'sinning'. In many cases careful investigation reveals that the person originally accused of anti–social behaviour has equally serious grievances against their accuser.

2.1   Fear Of Complaining

Charges and counter charges are not always brought out into the open. Some complainants fear retaliation and so feel unable to complain about neighbours. Or else they need confidentiality guaranteed and are unwilling to follow their complaint through to act as a witness if the landlord decides to take legal action.

'I'm a bit worried as I live on my own and these people are right opposite me – I wouldn't like them to think it was me. I've got a lot to worry about as it is ...'

People in this situation do not always trust their landlord to treat the matter completely confidentially and are afraid the neighbour will guess who has complained. Ironically, but not surprisingly, the more serious the problem, and the more criminal activity is involved, the more frightened tenants are likely to be about complaining.

'I know if I'd made a complaint and the housing association had approached him, I know he would put two and two together to work out it was me, as I'm the only other tenant on this floor. After seeing some of the characters he calls friends, I wouldn't like to cross them. I thought many times about complaining but I kept putting it off.... I want something to be done but would rather it wasn't me.'

These problems can cause extreme anxiety which the tenant feels helpless to remedy and may lead some tenants to move out rather than dare to complain.

'I'm a bit frightened really. What if it's discovered that it's me or my sons who have reported them? There's no one else lives here so they'd know, wouldn't they? What if I complain and the place is raided by police – I can't have that... But I feel I've got to do something soon. I don't know what to do for the best. I'm very worried... I'd rather move out first and then tell them, so there's no come–back on me from the people downstairs.'

Other tenants do not complain because they have little faith that the landlord can or will act to resolve the problem. Tenants report that some landlords are not interested in what they call 'clash of lifestyle' complaints. But some tenants admit that they do not know what the landlord can do about problems with neighbours, and many tenants do not realise they have any legal rights concerning nuisance (Tebay et al, 1986).

2.2   To Whom Do People Complain?

Despite these problems, those that do not complain when they have problems with a neighbour appear to be in a minority. The Salford University survey found that 76 per cent of tenants who had grievances against specific neighbours did voice a complaint. No other type of grievance had a higher rate of complaining: for instance only 48 per cent of tenants with grievances concerning the local environment or neighbourhood, and 57 per cent of all interviewed tenants who had had any sort of a grievance, voiced their complaint. All the tenants who voiced a complaint against a neighbour approached their landlord before contacting any other agencies who might further their complaint and only 16 per cent had contacted the 'offender' before contacting the landlord. As already stated, in some cases complainants feared reprisal if the 'offender' found out who had complained; others probably just could not face the unpleasantness of speaking to them directly. The incidence of this type of reluctance depended on the personality of the individuals concerned as well as on the subject of the complaint.

Many tenants interviewed in the Salford University survey also contacted outside agencies or individuals about a neighbour, after complaining to their landlord failed to resolve the problem. Most of these contacted the police, or less often the landlord contacted the police. In all these cases the problem had gone beyond a matter of irritation or annoyance to involve abuse or vandalism. There were also cases of tenants with grievances against neighbours seeking help from social workers or a family doctor, solicitors, councillors, environmental health departments and race equality officers. As we will see in Chapter 4, there is a need for effective liaison between landlords and other agencies over neighbour disputes.

2.3   Situations Which Give Rise To Neighbour Disputes

Clashes of life–style which so often cause neighbour disputes are particularly acute where people are brought into close proximity by high density housing.

• The Salford University interview survey found that 55 per cent of complainants with grievances against neighbours lived in flats, compared with 30 per cent of all interviewees.

• Residents of flats have the possibility of being disturbed by people living above or below them as well as to either side and there are problems of shared access which increase the opportunity for intimidation.

- Flat blocks are also the most likely type of property to be shared by households with very different lifestyles, such as elderly people and young single people or childless couples.

- Increasingly landlords cannot avoid housing children in flats. Yet dealing with young children in flat blocks is highly problematic for parents, in terms of noise, places to play, safety and supervision.

- A large proportion of complaints are made by older tenants about younger tenants and by women tenants about men.

But it is also true that prejudice may exacerbate complaining behaviour and make it difficult to disentangle the rights and wrongs of a situation. There is a fine dividing line, which is easily crossed, between justified indignation at anti–social behaviour, and prejudice about non–conforming behaviour, with associated reduced tolerance levels and a tendency towards complaints based on expected rather than actual behaviour. Typically, where clashes of life–styles are concerned, what one person sees as a legitimate complaint another sees as harassment.

'They complained about the volume of my music. I turned it down – I don't feel it was excessively loud – I've heard louder in friends' homes. The walls are thin and they carried on complaining. It got out of hand. They complained at everything I did – DIY even. I felt I couldn't move. They complained if I walked over the communal grass in front of the houses. It's because I'm a younger man and they probably see me as a trouble maker. I feel they were the trouble makers. I felt I was being harassed and it was my turn to complain'.

In some cases, notably racial harassment, the hostile behaviour of neighbours is clearly the subject of complaint rather than being the result of any behaviour on the part of the victim. The fact that such hostility exists towards ethnic and other minorities makes it an imperative that investigations of the problem take into account the views of both parties. We explore this further in Chapter 5.

Clash of Life Styles : The Case of A Housing Association

A change in allocation policy which produced a sudden clash in life–styles created an upsurge in dissatisfaction with neighbours amongst tenants of Housing Association B in one particular area. In fact, 70 per cent of tenants of Housing Association B interviewed by Salford University in that area had had at least one grievance about neighbours.

Housing Association B took over property from a New Town authority approximately two years prior to the interview survey. Some tenants who had previously rented from the New Town felt strongly that housing had been allocated to 'undesirable' tenants since the change of landlord with an associated change in letting policy. This was reflected in the high incidence of dissatisfaction with specific neighbours and with general nuisance created by local residents including vandalism, litter in communal areas, problems caused by dogs and car repairs. Several tenants had complained (either alone or in groups) about the lack of screening of applicants and that the housing association did not seem interested in problems caused by the types of tenants who were now being housed. These problems were largely a product of a clash of life–styles. Normal and acceptable behaviour according to the culture and standards of tenants moving into the area was unacceptable according to established patterns in the ex–New Town neighbourhoods.

2.4 Petitions And The Involvement Of Residents' Or Tenants' Associations

In some cases of serious behaviour, a tenant may be the subject of multiple complaints, group action or petitions. This may come about through individual action on the part of a number of tenants, ad hoc meetings, more formal meetings of residents or tenants associations or by organising petitions. Some tenants only find the courage to complain when they do so with others. Although petitions cannot be used as evidence if a case is taken to court, they give an indication of the strength of local opinion and may provide the names of people who would be willing to act as individual witnesses in a court case.

Tenants' and residents' associations can also be consulted when landlords are considering their policy or practice for dealing with neighbour disputes. For example tenants' groups supported Manchester City Council's recently implemented policy of using injunctions to deal with offenders in neighbour disputes.

However, it is not normally appropriate for tenants' groups to be involved in the handling of neighbour disputes. Many groups have a policy of not voicing any grievance against another tenant because of the possible conflict of interests and the problems of loss of confidentiality if a group of tenants are told the details of such a dispute. Tenants' groups tend to concentrate on more general aspects of environmental concern, although these may, by implication, involve criticisms of individual tenant behaviour, such as mending cars in the street, failure to control dogs etc.

2.5   Conclusion

Although the majority of tenants with grievances against a neighbour appear to voice their complaint to the landlord, a sizeable minority suffer in silence. In addition to these, some complaints are made reluctantly by tenants who fear retaliation if confidentiality is not maintained. Perhaps most important, the vast majority of people who complain to their landlord have not first spoken to their neighbour about the matter. As we have seen this reluctance or refusal to voice a grievance either to the neighbour or to the landlord is often most marked in the most extreme cases where harassment and violence are felt to be a real threat. It is therefore very important for social landlords to deal with neighbour disputes in a sensitive manner which encourages potential complainants to feel more confident about how the matter will be dealt with, helps them to negotiate either directly or indirectly with their neighbour, and makes them feel that they will receive support whatever is ultimately decided about the most appropriate action to be taken. The way in which neighbour disputes are dealt with needs to be publicised in a clear and simple form to reassure potential complainants about the reception and assistance they will receive. The following chapters deal with ways in which neighbour disputes are currently tackled and how practices can be made more effective.

Chapter 3
Current Approaches To Neighbour Disputes: Laissez Faire

In the previous chapter we saw that tenants need support and well understood structures to help them deal with disputes. How effective are landlords in this respect?

3.1 Excessive Reliance On Tenancy Agreements

Most landlords still rely solely on tenancy agreements to support their stance on neighbour disputes. This excessive reliance on enforcing tenancy agreements as the sole strategy for neighbour disputes unrealistically assumes that 'guilt' can be established and it gives aggrieved tenants an exaggerated view of the powers of the local authority or housing association to enforce tenancy agreements. A tenant is implicitly encouraged to demand that their neighbour is evicted or otherwise disciplined. Without any other description of what the landlord could offer, for instance mediation between the parties, tenants have nothing else to turn to than the 'enforcement of the tenancy' and no reason to suppose that this may not be enforceable or that the landlord will be reluctant to pursue a legalistic approach through to legal action. (Legal remedies and the reasons why social landlords hesitate to resort to them are discussed in Chapter 7).

Tenancy agreements are used to provide guidelines of what the landlord considers reasonable behaviour and tenants accused of causing a nuisance are referred to them. (The sorts of clauses that are commonly advocated are discussed in Section 7.3). The advantage of having such clauses in tenancy agreements is that if these conditions have been breached it is easier for housing officers to support their initial request that 'offenders' change their behaviour, and, if necessary, to pursue this with the threat of more drastic measures. In some cases it may be necessary to follow up unsuccessful attempts by housing officers or independent mediators to resolve a matter, by resorting to legal action or other types of sanctions.

In cases of racial harassment, the London Borough of Lambeth sends out strong warning letters to offenders outlining any contraventions of tenancy agreements, followed usually by a home visit from an estates officer and a Housing Advisor (Race Relations). These officials discuss incidents with offenders and warn them of the consequences should the offensive behaviour continue.

Occasionally, in the case of extreme behaviour, such as violent harassment, it will be felt appropriate to use legal action directly without attempting resolution by any other method.

However, the problem is that landlords are frequently unwilling to translate threats into action. Indeed the biggest criticism of the way in which social landlords currently deal with neighbour disputes is that if nothing is immediately resolved, few have any clear progression of intervention, either mediation, or, in the last resort, legal enforcement. They tend instead to leave the tenants to sort things out themselves.

Often the two parties in a neighbour dispute are merely urged to take notice of the tenancy agreement and to work out a solution but are not given any real assistance in doing this, even when it appears clear that they would not be able to resolve their problem without help. The result is frequently that the situation escalates.

'In dealing with conflicts between tenants, housing officers seem to have little faith in reconciliation. Their work almost always involves making tenants aware they are causing a nuisance but a settlement is rarely achieved as a result of tenants finding a compromise themselves. If tenants are not encouraged to reach such a compromise, their relationships are essentially unchanged. Indeed the involvement of the authority, especially if it is confrontational may incite resentment and further hostility. In this climate it is not altogether surprising that some disputes persist. What promises to be more effective is for tenants to reach an agreement acceptable to all those involved, even if that agreement amounts to nothing more than a 'cease–fire'. (Tebay et al, p.22).

Case Study: Laissez Faire and Lack of Consistency

A complaint was made to a housing association in July 1989 by a pensioner, Mr J, about Mr F's children. The initial complaint followed Mr F's son cycling on the footpath and nearly knocking Mr J over. Mr F overheard Mr J telling his son off and reacted by using abusive language. Mr J claimed that Mr F poked him, insulted his wife, threatened to harm him, his wife and home and stuck his face so close to Mr J that he was spitting on him. Mr J spat back! The end result was that Mr J slammed his door shut and Mr F kicked it in temper. The police were called but no action was taken.

Mr J made a complaint orally to a housing assistant and then put it in writing to the area housing manager. The area housing manager wrote to Mr J saying that Mr F had been charged for the minor damage caused to the door, told that threatening behaviour and wilful damage were not acceptable, but that no other action would be taken. Mr J wrote back to the assistant director of housing saying that he was 'absolutely disgusted at [the area housing manager's] attitude'. He quoted the tenants handbook as saying that action would be taken against any tenant found to be responsible for verbal abuse. Mr J also quoted the Housing Association's complaints procedure which says that, if discussing the complaint with your housing officer does not resolve it, you should complain in writing to the regional housing manager and then to the assistant director of housing. This letter was passed to the deputy regional housing manager to be dealt with. She replied to Mr J, reiterating the response of the area housing manager. The letter also asked Mr J to adopt a 'more flexible attitude' with local children. In a memo which accompanied a copy of this letter to the assistant director of housing, she stated that she thought it was 'a classic situation of a personality clash and it is unlikely that Mr F and Mr J will ever enjoy good relations'.

Mr J replied to the assistant director of housing saying that Mr F and his children were not open to reason. He reported more incidents in which Mr F's children deliberately caused a nuisance and used abusive language. He asked for action from the housing association. Shortly after this, in mid August, Mrs J wrote to the housing association, the Prime Minister and the local MP asking about their housing association's practice of housing older tenants near to young people. This letter was acknowledged by the regional housing manager. Two months later the local MP wrote a brief and seemingly uninterested letter to the assistant director of housing asking him to deal with the matter.

In September the assistant director of housing replied to Mr J's letter saying that the assistant housing manager had again spoken to Mr F who said that although his children were not responsible for the incidents complained about, he would tell them not to play outside Mr J's door. Mr F also said that it did not seem appropriate for the housing association to be involved in 'trivial complaints' between neighbours – the area housing manager supported this view. Mr J was advised to deal directly with Mr F and to remember that he lived in an area of three bedroomed family houses.

In October Mr J wrote to the assistant director of housing again, complaining that the problems were continuing, despite Mr F having told his children off in front of Mr J. He also said that Mr F was unapproachable and so dealing directly with him was not feasible. He stated that other tenants were considering moving because of the F family. The assistant director of housing replied reiterating that the problem should be taken up with Mr F and saying that 'The housing association is concerned with the welfare of its customers, but the misbehaviour of children is first and foremost the responsibility of their parents'. The Housing Association again informed Mr F that his children were causing concern.

In late December Mr J wrote to the area housing manager stating that he was afraid to deal directly with Mr F because Mr F couldn't control his temper and became abusive. A new area housing manager was in post and she replied that she would visit Mr J to discuss the case. After doing this she visited Mr F. No more was heard from either party: the shift in approach to be slightly more mediatory appears to have successfully resolved the dispute – or at least the two parties gave up complaining to the association about each other.

Until this last stage the housing association handled this complaint at arm's length with very little flexibility and tact. For a long time they did not alter their original response, despite continued complaints from Mr J and the fact that other tenants in the area left because of Mr F. The housing association did not appear to consider taking action to enforce the tenancy agreement or to appreciate that Mr J would probably fear retaliation if he dealt directly with Mr F. Mr J had referred to the tenants handbook and tenancy agreement and used various channels to gain redress, all to no avail. It is possible that the matter would have blown over if Mr J had been less determined, however less persistent tenants may well have suffered in silence. Although several different housing officers dealt with the complaint they had communicated with each other, giving some continuity to the handling of the grievance. However, the standard of record keeping was not sufficient to show exactly what the new area housing manager did which was successful in stopping the complaints or indeed whether the matter was resolved to the tenants' approval.

3.2   Moving The 'Perpetrator' Or The 'Victim'

When disputes have escalated, landlords frequently, and understandably, resort to transfers. But, in England and Wales, transfers have to be with the consent of the party involved; the only way in which a 'compulsory transfer' can be carried out is through eviction and rehousing. (In Scotland it is, however, possible to enforce a transfer. See Legal Appendix 3.) As we discuss later (Chapter 7), eviction is a slow and difficult procedure and is rarely used. In the Salford study, most of the housing organisations said that they would prefer to transfer an offender than seek an eviction. However, in reality it is much more likely to be the person who is complaining about offensive behaviour who accepts a transfer.

The most detailed evidence about the use of transfers in neighbour disputes relates to racial harassment cases. A survey of thirty one London boroughs found that, though a majority had policies on racial harassment, only ten had actually taken matters to court – some twenty five cases in all (Legal Action Group, 1990). Most authorities resorted to transferring the victims of the offensive behaviour. In Camden, for example, according to a 1988 survey, between 30 and 40 transfers were made annually in consequence of racial harassment – this compared with four cases between 1986 and 1990 where court action was taken against perpetrators of harassment (London Borough of Camden, 1988).

Transfers of this sort actually reward those whose behaviour is offensive for they advance their aim of forcing out ethnic minority tenants from an area.

Case Study: The Case Of A Victim Of Harassment Who Felt Driven To Accepting A Transfer

Ms T, a local authority tenant, was the victim of harassment from her next door neighbour, Mr C. He initially complained to her about her dog but followed this up by verbally abusing her, breaking her windows and throwing bricks at her when she was in the garden. Ms T had a high fence erected between their gardens but Mr C broke it down. Mr C also harassed and intimidated other local residents including previous tenants of Ms T's home.

Ms T complained to the housing department about Mr C's behaviour. Housing officers said that all they could do was to talk to him. They interviewed Mr C who denied all the allegations of causing harassment. After this Ms T claimed that his behaviour was worse than before. She contacted the police who simply advised her to call a truce. She then contacted a solicitor who wrote to the council on her behalf. When the council did not take steps to resolve the problem, Ms T was advised to proceed with a court action against Mr C. Mr C was bound over for two years but continued to harass her.

After this Ms T accepted a transfer from the council although she felt that moving away implied that she was at fault. She was unwilling to live with the aggressive behaviour of Mr C for any longer and also feared that any further intervention from housing staff might again cause an escalation of the matter.

In cases of anti–social behaviour, transfers, like evictions, merely move the problem to another place and expose a new neighbour to possible dispute. For this reason, where threats and persuasion fail, some housing authorities are resorting to different remedies, such as injunctions, to tackle the behaviour itself (see Chapter 7). However, in cases where problems are caused by personality clashes between particular individuals, whose anti–social behaviour is directed solely at each other, the matter may be most readily resolved by moving one of them.

However, some local authority officers consider that over–readiness by a complainant to accept a transfer weakens the complainant's case. Some allegations of nuisance by neighbours may be put forward as a disguised transfer request by a complainant, and thus all such allegations should be carefully investigated to check that they have not been 'massaged' to give the matter undue prominence.

3.3 Conclusion : The Lack Of A Coherent And Effective Strategy

Currently many tenants feel let down by landlords who appear to do little to deal with neighbour disputes. They are especially resentful where the landlord has a declared policy on nuisance, breach of tenancy agreements or on specific clauses in the tenancy agreement but does not enforce it. Tenants in these circumstances become very disillusioned and may well give up attempts to vindicate their rights.

Many tenants complain that their landlords attribute problems entirely to the 'mixing of age groups' and say that tenants 'will have to put up with it', this despite the fact that two neighbours can sometimes come to blows with each other. One housing association in the Salford study told the researchers that there was usually nothing they could do because 'it takes two neighbours to cause trouble'. In effect, like many other landlords, they were saying that if clear blame was not attributed to one family, they would do nothing. This, in effect, rules out addressing the majority of neighbour disputes. It also means that, without a neutral party to help, warring neighbours are often unable to reach agreement. They need help in resolving their differences. This is why active mediation is increasingly seen as a constructive option which is much more effective and appropriate for a large number of neighbour disputes.

In the following chapters we go on to consider a more hands–on approach to neighbour disputes, recognising that solutions are difficult but not impossible, and that negotiated compromises may be the answer to some problems, while others may inevitably end in legal action. But whichever route is taken, the landlord needs to pursue that route effectively.

Illustration by Malcolm Willett

23

Chapter 4
A Coherent Approach
To Neighbour Disputes

As we have seen in Chapter 3, neighbour disputes currently tend to be dealt with in a very ad hoc way, by both local authorities and housing associations, depending more on the skills of particular staff in personal relationships than thought–out policies, procedures and training provided by the landlord. The result is that most landlords tend to swing between a legalistic and 'laissez faire' approach which can exacerbate rather than solve problems. This in turn tends to give staff the view that neighbour disputes are intrinsically 'insoluble', which reinforces the laissez–faire approach. However, there are a growing number of notable exceptions and we will be drawing on their experience to demonstrate what can be done.

4.1 A Strategy For Neighbour Disputes

As the Institute of Housing stresses in its *Housing Management Standards Manual* (IoH, 1993), landlords need, first and foremost, a coherent strategy in relation to neighbour disputes and, second, effective implementation of that strategy.

The following elements should be included in such a strategy and plan for its implementation.

- Preventive measures – through the design, layout and management of dwellings and their surroundings; ensuring that suitable legal remedies are available if required; involving tenants' and residents' groups; briefing of residents (both tenants and home–owners) on expectations of them; careful allocations etc.

- Formulation and publication of policies and procedures to cover:

  –the range of action that the landlord is willing to take and in what circumstances: including mediation, transfers and court action;

  –the identification of neighbour disputes (as opposed to other types of complaint) and deciding upon appropriate action;

  –investigation of the situation to ascertain the views of all parties and advise them on courses of action, making it easy for customers to report problems.

- Arrangements for inter–agency and inter–departmental co–operation including the resourcing and recruitment of staff or outside agencies to undertake investigations, advice, mediation, negotiation or court action.

- Training of officers.

- Keeping records of each case, monitoring progress and reporting to committee members.

- Setting the timescales for action and avoiding unnecessary delay which could lead to the escalation of problems.

We will now go on to discuss the factors which should be taken into account within each of these elements when formulating and implementing a strategy for dealing with neighbour disputes. The different types of action which can be taken and how they can be most effectively implemented are examined in more detail in subsequent chapters.

4.2   Preventive Measures

Although it is hard to predict precisely what circumstances will lead to neighbour disputes, landlords should take sensible preventive measures. Action which might prevent neighbour disputes would be cost effective, reducing the amount of time housing officers spend dealing with such disputes. It would also improve the quality of life of tenants, leading to a reduction in the stress and aggravation they experience and encouraging the development of more positive and tolerant attitudes towards neighbours and housing staff.

4.2.1 Property And Estate Design, Layout And Management.

Many neighbour disputes have their origins in the nature and layout of the property itself and the layout and management of its surroundings. For example:

- Complaints about noise from children playing outside can be reduced if safe play areas are provided which are not immediately adjacent to housing occupied by elderly people or childless couples. Supervised or organised activities in school holidays can also reduce this problem.

- Sometimes neglect of gardens is a cause of friction. Some landlords and tenants' groups try to reduce this by providing help with gardening, garden tool lending services etc. Similarly, if landlords make efforts to ensure that adequate litter and refuse disposal services are provided and communal areas are well maintained, people may be more inclined to care for their neighbourhood and, even if some do not, the majority will not be so badly affected.

- Landlords can help to control the problems caused by dogs by creating dog free areas with adequate fencing and security to keep dogs out, especially in childrens' play areas.

- Complaints about noise, especially those caused by general household noise rather than loud music, would decrease if sound proofing were improved. Where new dwellings are being built, particular attention should be given to the layout of dwellings in relation to each other, for instance avoiding rooms with noisy household machinery against party walls which adjoin living or sleeping areas and in flat blocks avoiding living rooms above bedrooms. Buffer zones provided by passages can be particularly effective, as can backing kitchens or utility rooms onto each other.

- In existing flats, remedies may be more limited but tenants could be encouraged or even assisted to carpet their dwellings, although in most cases such a measure is likely to be far too expensive for either landlord or tenant (Tebay et al, 1986).

4.2.2 Ensuring That All Suitable Legal Measures Are Available If Required

In Chapter 7 we discuss in some detail the legal powers that landlords have to deal with anti–social behaviour. To use some of these, landlords have to devise their own forms of regulation. In particular landlords need to design suitable tenancy agreements. But local authority landlords may also wish to use other powers such as housing byelaws (discussed further in Legal Appendix 1.2.) or covenants on the sale of Right to Buy property (discussed in Legal Appendix 1.3). The value of such measures is that they not only provide the authority with greater powers to deal with problems of nuisance, harassment and other forms of anti–social behaviour when they arise, but also, through publicity about the standards of behaviour expected, probably provide some deterrent effect before the event. Authorities that use covenants on Right to Buy property see them as a way of stressing equality of rights and duties between tenures in respect of neighbour relationships.

4.2.3 Involving Tenants

Tenants' and residents' associations can very usefully be involved in:

• helping to design and give active support to tenancy and licence agreements and covenants to cover nuisance, damage and harassment;

• devising policies and facilitating procedures for responding to anti–social behaviour, for reporting incidents and supporting victims of harassment.

With adequate support when there are very difficult cases, tenants can usually be more effective in creating neighbourly behaviour and good relationships in their local 'patch' than the landlord can ever be. However, there will always be some cases that are not amenable to such an approach and in some estates levels of intimidation and violence completely undermine such an approach.

4.2.4 Advising and Informing Tenants

In general when people take up a tenancy they should be advised about problems which occur in particular situations or affect particular groups of tenants, such as those living in flats. Much annoyance is caused unwittingly and some would be prevented if tenants were asked to behave considerately and follow general guidelines.

- Landlords could publicise and promote the pet owners' code of practice drawn up by JACOPIS, ADC, AMA and the IoH (Morton, 1991.)

- Tenants could be advised about the levels of noise that are likely to be troublesome to neighbours and be advised to refrain from playing loud music or slamming doors, especially at night. In flats, wearing slippers indoors can avoid a lot of disturbance.

- Newsletters could be used to remind tenants of the need to behave considerately and tolerantly towards their neighbours. Neighbours should also be encouraged to talk to each other about problems before they escalate. Mentioning noise to a neighbour should be accepted as a sensible approach rather than an offensive one.

- Where it is known in advance that someone is planning an event that will cause a nuisance, for example a pay party, they could be visited before the event to see if problems could be avoided.

- Information also needs to be given about the disputes policy and the fact that the landlord will endeavour, without taking sides, to resolve neighbour disputes and, where it occurs, to curb anti–social behaviour.

- The terms of byelaws, tenancy and licence agreements and covenants about issues which frequently cause annoyance, such as keeping dogs and carrying out car repairs, should also be clearly laid out and publicised to make people aware of the landlord or local authority's expectations.

- The penalties for breaching agreements and byelaws should also be publicised. Some authorities claim that there is a particular preventive value in taking well–publicised legal action against recalcitrant tenants because other potentially disruptive tenants see this as evidence of the serious intent of the landlord in enforcing reasonable behaviour.

4.2.5 Allocations Policies

Since many neighbour disputes are caused by conflicting life styles, one solution in the longer term would appear to be selective allocation. For instance, it has been suggested that selective allocation, with the introduction of young singles blocks, maturity blocks and warden–controlled schemes, could almost halve the number of complaints (Tebay, 1986). However, while segregation might reduce inter–generational conflict, it will not affect intra–generational differences due to varied lifestyles within the segregated groups.

While some degree of age segregation may be sensible and popular, especially in flat blocks, solutions based on selective allocations should be treated with care. Some complaints by neighbours are based on prejudices about, for instance, black households or female single parents. It would be both inequitable and illegal to allow prejudice and stereotyping to determine what choice of housing people receive. Judgements of this type have been one of the major causes of segregated 'sink estates' where the most vulnerable and powerless invariably find themselves placed next to the most disruptive.

The Dilemmas of Allocations Officers

Allocations officers have many conflicting pressures on them when they make decisions about offers of property. For instance, one officer described a typical case in which he decided not to offer an unemployed single parent with several children a particular property because of the number of home owners in that street who might complain. The 'history' sheet in the case papers contained a reference to the need for social work support and there were a few letters from neighbours complaining about the woman's 'unruly' children. The officer who was vetting a transfer offer which had been made to her commented as follows:

'They've caused a lot of trouble, so they're not really suitable for the offer... in this road there are some owner occupiers and there has already been trouble ... so we don't really want another problem family in there causing more trouble. So I'm not going to sign this one (the offer). I shall send it back to the other area and say we can't have this family'.

This illustrates how labelling a family as 'a problem' may affect their chances of being allocated a particular property and how the officer's concern to avoid management problems can over–ride other factors such as equal opportunities, in the allocation decision (Henderson and Karn, 1987, p.268–9).

In general, though some preventive measures can be taken, landlords have to recognise that some degree of clashing life–styles is inevitable and that any amount of 'social engineering' cannot prevent it. As we will see later, the only way forward lies in 'giving mediation a chance' and if that fails, resorting to legal powers. There can be no total prevention or total cure.

4.3   Formulation And Publication Of Appropriate Policies And Procedures

4.3.1 The Range Of Action The Landlord Is Willing To Take

Despite the Ombudsman issuing guidelines about approaches to neighbour disputes (Laws, 1990) most housing authorities and associations do not even have an explicitly formulated and publicised strategy about neighbour disputes.

* Only eight of the thirty–nine authorities surveyed by Grant (1987) had a specific policy statement on neighbour disputes. The corollary of this is of course that they had no policy statement to communicate to tenants or their own officers.

* Of the eight in Grant's study who had a policy statement, six included explanations of their stance in their tenants' handbook. These included explanations of the most frequent causes of complaints, and under what conditions and how the authority would intervene.

Yet it is vital that tenants (and owners) have a clear understanding of both the expectations of landlords and the local authority about what constitutes unneighbourly behaviour, what action the landlord or local authority is willing to take in helping to resolve problems and what sanctions can be, and are likely to be, invoked if this type of behaviour persists. Such information will both have some preventive influence and will also encourage people to approach the organisation for help.

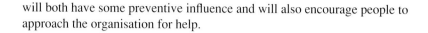

St Helens Metropolitan Borough Council has produced guidance notes for staff receiving and dealing with nuisance complaints. These take the form of seven performance standards, with details of how each should be implemented. Subjects covered include:

• providing accessible contact points for receiving complaints;

• deciding on suitable courses of action and investigating complaints;

• staff attitudes to tenants involved in disputes;

• when it may be appropriate to involve other agencies.

Local office staff receive training which includes applying these guidelines, counselling skills and basic legal knowledge.

For further details contact Donal Hughes, Area Estate Manager at St Helens Metropolitan Borough Council, Telephone: 0744–820303.

Manchester City Council have recently produced a detailed manual for staff on dealing with neighbour disputes. Details of this are given in Section 4.5.

4.3.2 Identifying Neighbour Disputes And Deciding On Appropriate Action

One factor which reduces the ease and efficiency with which most landlords deal with neighbour disputes is that they use the same complaints procedure to deal with all complaints, including neighbour disputes. But clearly a complaint about a delayed repair or incorrect rent bill should be approached very differently from a neighbour dispute or a bad relationship between a tenant and their local housing officer. To adopt an identical approach can result in complaints procedures becoming overloaded with neighbour and other disputes, which are often complex, take longer to resolve than other complaints and require very different approaches. Thus, if disputes which require mediation are identified and separated out at reception into a special route, all types of complaints can be dealt with more efficiently and effectively (Figure 2).

As complaints come in, the intake process should be capable of first establishing what the basic details of the grievance are as presented by the complainant. To be most effective, and to gain the trust and confidence of the complainant at this early stage, the intake process should offer a variety of options, and develop a mutual agreement with the complainant about the option which matches his or her complaint with the most appropriate style of resolution process.

As Figure 2 suggests, there is a fundamental initial decision to make. Is this a complaint about the landlord's services or a dispute between neighbours? This is an important distinction to make:

'Action needed to solve disputes is likely to be quite different from that needed to deal with complaints' (Simpson and McCarthy, 1993).

Figure 2   Channelling Complaints

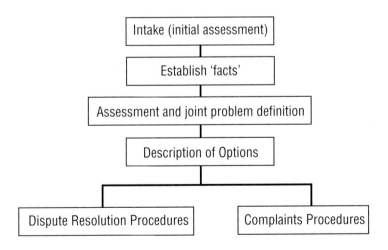

Neighbour disputes do not normally start as complaints against the landlord, but they frequently develop in that direction if they are not satisfactorily dealt with in the view of the complainant.

The Local Government Ombudsman in fact received a complaint about one London Housing Authority because tenants were unhappy with the lack of effective procedures for dealing with neighbour disputes. Subsequently, this authority has developed procedures which include plans to set up a mediation service pilot scheme.

Procedures for dealing with neighbour disputes need to be flexible. Facts are often difficult to establish, and disputants experience shifting emotions which cause them to modify demands and select different methods of resolution from those originally decided upon. Intake staff require:

• an understanding of the nature of disputes and disputants' behaviour;

• the ability to listen actively, collecting information tactfully and gaining the trust and confidence of the complainant;

• full awareness of the resolution options available in their own department, in other departments within the same organisation, or in outside agencies;

• working practices which facilitate a constructive, rapid, sensitive referral where necessary;

• support structures which enable consultation with other staff on matters of policy and practice.

The nature, degree of intensity and significance of the dispute need to be assessed at intake, to decide upon the appropriate nature and timescale of response. The timescale will depend partly on urgency and partly on the staffing resources available. But the fact that a dispute seems trivial does not necessarily mean that it does not require prompt action. Many complaints about neighbours are relatively minor and can be resolved by quick and decisive action from housing assistants. If appropriate action is taken to deal with such disputes they can be prevented from escalation into something more serious. Front–line staff must be given sufficient authority as well as guidelines to deal with these cases.

A Framework for Categorising Neighbour Complaints

A framework which gives guidelines for categorising complaints has been developed and piloted in the course of a recent research project. (The response times would need to be decided upon by each housing organisation depending on their situation).

Category 1: *Complaints which concern clear breaches of the tenancy conditions and which require a response only from housing management.* Examples would be: damage to property; neglect of a garden; failure to clean a communal area; running a business from the property.

Category 2: *Complaints which require a response from housing management, but in conjunction with other agencies or departments.* Examples include: harassment or domestic violence where tenants are victims (the police, social services and voluntary agencies might all be involved); disruptive behaviour by someone with a mental illness or mental disability (mental health agencies and social services might be consulted); nuisance associated with drug or alcohol abuse (a range of voluntary and statutory agencies could be involved).

Category 3: *Complaints which are not housing matters, but which require initial advice from housing staff, followed by referral to other agencies or departments.* Examples include: noise nuisance (an environmental health matter); criminal behaviour, such as theft from empty properties or harassment of people who are not tenants (both are police matters); neighbour disputes which arise from clashes of life styles or simple personal dislike (referral might be to a mediation service or to an alternative landlord).

The decision about where to locate neighbour complaints within the above framework will not always be clear cut and will depend on the judgement of the housing officer concerned.

This framework has been developed as part of a research project studying the management of neighbour complaints in social housing. The research has been carried out by Aldbourne Associates and funded by the Joseph Rowntree Foundation. A practitioner's handbook dealing with the management of neighbour complaints in social housing and setting out a

policy and procedure framework is being published in 1993. For further
details contact Sue Farrant, telephone 0635 551297.

There is a variety of procedures and techniques which can be used for the
resolution of neighbour disputes, once they have been channelled into a
specialist service (Figure 3).

Figure 3: Dispute Resolution Continuum

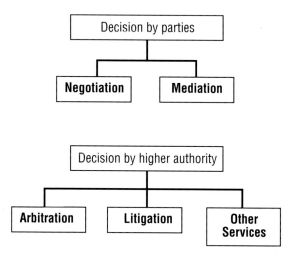

Adapted from Slaikeu, 1989

Negotiation and mediation both leave the final decision to the parties
themselves but mediation introduces a third party to assist in reaching
agreement. Arbitration, litigation and other types of sanctions rely on higher
authority, an arbitrator or judge, to impose a solution. Any of these strategies
may be appropriate for a particular dispute at a particular time but successful
resolution is most likely to occur where the parties to a dispute have agreed to
use or abide by the chosen strategy. Negotiation and mediation allow a more
constructive approach to dispute resolution and result in a solution which the
parties have agreed to abide by or work towards rather than demanding that
they accept an imposed solution. However, these strategies also require the
parties to have more commitment to reach and abide by a solution.

Mediation is particularly suitable for use in neighbour disputes where subjective differences in opinion are involved and where there is room for negotiation in a controlled situation. Some local authorities and housing associations have recognised the difficulty of incorporating neighbour disputes into other aspects of their work and have set up, supported or used independent mediation or neighbour dispute services. Chapters 5 and 6 discuss the use of mediation in the resolution of neighbour disputes.

4.3.3 Investigation To Ascertain The Views Of All Parties And Making It Easy For Customers To Report Problems

Most local authorities and housing associations agree that the initial action of the landlord is investigation and the collection of information from both parties.

- In most housing authorities both parties to a neighbour complaint are visited, usually by a housing assistant (Grant, 1987).

- Where the complaint is found to be justified the visits are most often followed by a letter to the 'offender' explaining that they are in breach of the tenancy agreement, requesting greater consideration in the future, and in some cases warning of possible legal action against them if they do not comply.

- With persistent problems, it is also common practice for the complainant to be asked to keep a written record of precisely when the nuisance occurs and what form it takes. In addition to providing information to the landlord, if legal action is taken such evidence is often required by courts before granting orders.

- Some housing organisations provide 'Nuisance Record Forms' but few of these are helpfully designed. This is clearly an area where tenants could be given greater assistance.

However, it should be noted that in some cases, to avoid exacerbating the situation, home visits may have either to be avoided or else made surreptitiously to the complainant only.

Some organisations surveyed by Salford University insisted that neighbour complaints were put in writing even if other categories of complaint were accepted verbally. The reasons given for this were that:

• a written statement may be needed as evidence at a later date, and

• it will act as a safeguard against slanderous statements which will later be denied if the case is taken to court.

However, some tenants are not willing to write down their grievance against fellow tenants, feeling that to do so could make them more vulnerable to retaliation. Indeed this view was shared by the chair of one housing association management committee, who said that putting a neighbour complaint in writing was a sure way to escalate a dispute which could have been resolved by a visit from a housing assistant.

Initial complaints about neighbours should be accepted orally over the telephone or in person. If necessary, formal statements can be written by the complainant or dictated to staff at a later date. It must be possible for people to complain in a way which is convenient and easy for them.

Sensibly many landlords, before they will act upon neighbour complaints, ask the complainant to discuss their grievance with the offending neighbour, if at all possible, pointing out that very often the person complained about has a story as plausible as that of the complainant.

'[The neighbour] may not be aware that a nuisance is being caused and may be very apologetic once he/she is aware that you are unhappy with the situation. It is better for everyone if you can sort the matter out on a neighbourly basis.' (Mendip District Council, p.2)

However, some landlords appear to have too inflexible an approach about insisting on complainants contacting neighbours before they will take any action. As we have seen, in many cases tenants are unwilling to contact the 'offender' directly for fear of retaliation; indeed in the Salford survey only 16 per cent of complainants had done so. While, in more trivial disputes, those who talk things over with their neighbour may avoid escalating conflict, it has to be recognised that many conflicts are not of this type and too rigid a requirement for tenants to discuss the matter with neighbours, unaccompanied by any other person, may be neither acceptable, productive nor even in some cases, safe. It may merely have the effect of deterring people from complaining to the landlord at all. In these cases particularly, some form of mediation is needed at a very early stage.

4.4   Inter-Agency And Inter-Departmental Co-operation

In dealing effectively and efficiently with neighbour disputes, social landlords will need to work with other agencies including the police, environmental health departments and social services departments. It is important that there is an agreed strategy with these organisations and well established procedures for referral, liaison and coordination of action and that officers are briefed about these. It will be helpful if links can be made with named officers in other organisations who can be contacted either to discuss a case and obtain advice or to request action by another agency. It is important that records of action taken and decisions made are kept by each agency. The housing organisation should keep records of when other agencies were contacted, what they did, and what they achieved.

Manchester City Council housing department has recently taken action to improve links with other agencies. They have a referral system with the police and have drawn up guidelines which detail when the police should be involved in disputes. These are being used on a pilot basis. They have also devised forms on which complainants can indicate whether they agree to the involvement of the police or other agancies. In addition they work closely with the Council's other departments, including the legal and environmental health departments, when this is appropriate in dealing with a dispute.

The agencies with which it will most often be appropriate to liaise are:

*   The police in cases where the criminal law has been broken, for example in cases of violence, harassment or drug dealing, or in other cases of nuisance or noise incidents with which the police have powers to deal but where no criminal charges are made.

- Environmental health departments which are responsible for dealing with noise control and incidents which give rise to situations which pose a health hazard, including vermin, the accumulation of rubbish and problems caused by animals, notably for ensuring that dog waste is safely removed.

- Dog warden services and relevant animal charities to deal with problems of pets and strays.

- Social services departments who will most often be involved if children or elderly people are thought to be at risk or if there are problems arising from the behaviour of elderly people or those suffering from or recovering from mental health, drug abuse or alcohol problems.

- A variety of care agencies when problems are caused by vulnerable tenants whose inappropriate behaviour affects neighbours. Such situations are increasing as social landlords house more of these people, in particular those discharged into the community under Care in the Community policies. These people are often unable to participate in mediation or negotiated approaches to dispute resolution. Landlords have the possibility of involving care agencies to avoid legal action to deal with problems which cannot be resolved by their own informal methods. One housing association contacted during the Salford University research was devising a policy for seeking the involvement of care agencies when the tenant concerned had not agreed to this. Care agencies that the association had been involved with felt that they should become involved when necessary because this was in the tenants' interests and offered possibilities for reaching a constructive solution when the alternative would often be legal action against vulnerable tenants with the possibility of their home being repossessed.

- Local authority planning departments may be involved where disputes concern unauthorised alterations. Planning regulations may also prohibit the running of businesses from dwellings or keeping pets and livestock.

- Other organisations such as advice agencies, GPs and solicitors may be involved in disputes if they are asked for advice and assistance, most often by individuals, but possibly also on the recommendation of the landlord.

- Councillors may be contacted about neighbour disputes by tenants of housing associations as well as of local authorities. Councillors may advise complainants, contact the relevant agencies on behalf of complainants, or may go further than this to become involved in coordinating action to resolve the problem. The level of involvement will depend both on the subject and seriousness of the complaint and on the individual councillor.

In some cases the agency which is first alerted to the problem will not take direct action itself but will refer the case on to another more appropriate one. This obviously depends on the nature of the problem, the powers of the organisations concerned and on what action is decided upon.

Clearly housing associations with less powers of their own, smaller legal advice facilities and no environmental health powers or staff, will have particular need to establish inter–agency links of this sort. As we discuss later, landlords may also find it preferable to pay a 'retainer' to an independent mediation agency rather than attempt to develop their own (see Chapter 6).

4.5 Staff Training

The selection, training and support of staff is a key part of the dispute resolution process, contributing to the number of viable options which can be offered for the resolution of disputes. In practice, most authorities admit that front–line staff, including concierges, receptionists, clerks, estate managers and housing officers, do not have all the appropriate skills and that they are hampered by lack of training and support.

> In the study of Birmingham City Housing Department only one of 21 housing assistants surveyed had received formal training in dealing with neighbour nuisance. However seventy one per cent thought that they would benefit from training and exchanging experiences with officers from other areas (Tebay et al, 1986, p.17).

Often only the most experienced officers, who have learned largely by trial and error, are able to channel complaints effectively into the best resolution procedure (which often means spending a considerable amount of time dealing with the complainants themselves). In addition, housing officer's education and training has had very little emphasis on the taking and giving of evidence, as compared with the training of environmental health officers.

However, a growing number of housing organisations, notably local authorities, are now recognising the particular skills needed to deal with neighbour disputes and are providing training. The types of training needed are quite diverse, namely:

• current policies regarding nuisance
• counselling skills
• conciliation and mediation
• the role and respective powers of other agencies
• legal aspects of nuisance
• taking evidence
• giving evidence in court
• the needs of ethnic minorities

While training is essential, it has to be recognised that the capacity of staff to offer complainants a more meaningful service is also hampered by the paucity of effective remedies at their disposal, and the inappropriateness of certain legal action, such as seeking eviction, for many of the disputes they encounter.

....

In 1992 Manchester City Council launched a programme of training for housing officers on dealing with neighbour disputes. This took the form of one day of training using both an external trainer and an internally produced manual *Solving Neighbour Problems*.

The manual supports a conciliatory approach 'rather than confrontation'. It includes details of:

• the Council's procedure for dealing with neighbour disputes;
• interview techniques, including guidelines on interviewing both the complainant and the alleged offender;
• records which should be kept;
• how to decide on a course of action.

The manual goes on to give details of legal action which may be appropriate when a conciliatory approach does not lead to an improvement.

Training was initially given to the 52 team leaders, will move on to include the deputy team leaders and should later be given in an amended form to all the neighbourhood officers. The Council is also hoping to be able to give some training in mediation to equip officers with the skills to conduct meetings with both parties to a dispute present.

Solving Neighbour Problems is available at a price of £130 plus p & p. Telephone 061–234–4722 for details.

Some further examples of staff training initiatives are given in chapter 6.

....

4.6 Monitoring

The monitoring of complaints includes:

- keeping a careful record of individual complaints made;

- analysing aggregated information about complaints to produce data which can be used in policy and practice reform;

- presenting periodic statistical and activity reports to committee.

Currently many housing organisations do not carry out any logging of complaints or disputes, merely adding letters or comments to property files. Yet logging is a central element of any complaints strategy and should be undertaken on a systematic basis. All complaints received and decisions made by the organisation should be recorded. Monitoring can only take place if information is systematically passed through the organisation.

Information technology can be usefully employed in the collection and categorisation of data. Most organisations have currently neglected to develop the use of computerised logging and monitoring systems to store this type of information about complaints in a standardised and easily accessible way. However, some organisations have recently installed computerised complaints recording and monitoring systems – either systems which have been developed 'in–house' or commercially produced systems.

....

Case Study : Computerised Monitoring

Wolverhampton Metropolitan Borough Council has recently begun to use an in–house computer system to record and monitor complaints about council services. This system is currently used only for complaints about the council, not those about third parties. (For example, if a customer complained about a neighbour this would not be recorded, but if the council failed to act on the request to deal with the problem, and the person complained about this, a formal complaint would then be recorded.)

Such a system could clearly be equally applicable to neighbour complaints.

In the Wolverhampton system a Complaints Recording Officer in each department is responsible for ensuring that every complaint is recorded on the computer system, acknowledged and actioned, although this system does not include records of complaints made by telephone or in person which are resolved 'on the spot'. Any action taken is recorded on the computer so that the system can also be used to monitor progress, ensure that agreed time–scales are met and that the complainant is kept informed. Standard letters to complainants can be generated by the computer system. As well as calling up data about individual complaints, it is possible to generate lists of selected information such as name of complainant, subject or category of complaint, section dealing with the matter and outcome of investigations. The system can produce reminders of overdue complaints – those which have not been dealt with within the specified time limit. The Complaints Recording Officer is also responsible for producing information and statistics necessary for reports to committees and management teams.

....

An up–to–date record of action taken is particularly important in neighbour disputes because these are frequently difficult to resolve, require visits to both disputants and may require action or monitoring over longer periods of time than most complaints about, for example, maintenance and repairs. If the problem is passed on to more senior staff, those who specialise in dealing with neighbour disputes or other organisations, it is important that an accurate record of what has already occurred is available.

The following basic details should be recorded:

• the date the complaint was received;

- who received the initial complaint;
- the method of complaint (written, telephone, visit, petition, etc);
- the names and addresses of the parties to the dispute;
- for equal opportunities purposes, the ethnicity, age and gender of the parties;
- any information about levels of violence or threatening behaviour;
- the key issues involved in the dispute;
- action taken on the matter;
- outcome.

It is important that records of action taken in neighbour disputes are detailed and that they are descriptive, concentrating on fact not opinion, interpretation or the assumptions of the interviewer. These records need to include:

- details of conversations and copies of letters between housing officers and tenants;

- details of other agencies' involvement;

- the date at which another agency took over responsibility for acting to resolve a dispute;

- an easily accessible summary of methods used in each case. It should be possible to see, for example, how many cases were referred to a mediation service, how many were resolved by the efforts of housing officers and how often the various types of legal remedy were used.

- particularly when new methods of dealing with disputes are being implemented, it may be useful to keep a simple and easily accessible record of how many hours of officers' time are taken up by disputes in order to assess the most effective use of staff resources.

At the level of the individual case, accurate records:

- will allow informed decisions about how to progress with the case;

- form the basis of evidence if legal action is taken.

Analysis of the aggregated material should also enable housing officers and committee members to:

- assess which remedies are most effective and cost effective in the long term from the point of view of all those involved;

- consider whether certain methods of resolution were especially suitable for particular categories of dispute;

- examine how effective the current procedures are in resolving neighbour dispute and whether officers are adhering to guidelines;

- yield information on the subject and incidence of neighbour disputes which can be used to help reduce the occurrence of situations which are prone to give rise to such complaints.

So information about neighbour disputes can be used to the benefit of the housing organisation as well as aiding efficient action to resolve individual disputes.

4.7 Timescales

Neighbour complaints should, like any other complaint, be acknowledged on receipt so that the complainant knows the matter is being dealt with and has the name and details of how to contact an officer who is investigating the case or co–ordinating action. Many organisations now have published time limits within which they will acknowledge and respond to complaints. For neighbour complaints it may be more difficult to specify when action will be completed. It will usually be necessary to visit at least two parties to the dispute at least once. It may be necessary to give the disputants time to consider suggested action, such as taking part in mediation or modifying behaviour or to wait for other agencies to act. However, it should be possible to indicate a time limit after which, if the matter has not been resolved, the complainant will be sent a progress report indicating what has been done and what the next steps will be. Obviously, neighbour disputes vary greatly in their urgency depending on, for example, whether violence or threatening behaviour is involved. Where both parties to a dispute are working towards a mutually agreeable solution, they should always be made aware of what will happen next and when this is likely to occur.

4.8   Implications Of CCT

There is a risk that local authorities will have their reluctance to take a more
pro–active role in neighbour disputes reinforced by the difficulty of
specifying, in a CCT contract, the resolution of neighbour disputes and in
particular mediation. The situation is exacerbated by the fact that, as most
landlords have not so far been active in relation to dispute resolution, they do
not have the past experience upon which to base requirements for their
contractors. At the time of writing, the authors had not found any authority
that had completed the specification of responses to neighbour disputes as
part of a contract. Several including Cambridge are however developing
drafts (see below.) There is a need for collaborative work on model
agreements if even the most forward looking landlords and contractors are
not to be tempted to opt out of dealing with neighbour disputes.

In preparing for such a task, Manchester's training document, *Solving
Neighbour Problems*, and, at a less detailed level, the Institute of Housing's
guidance in its *Housing Management Standards Manual* (IoH, 1993) provide
good starting points, though they do not profess to provide CCT contracts.
Management of Neighbours Complaints in Social Housing, by Aldbourne
Associates, is also helpful in classifying disputes with a view to specifying
response times.

....

Office Procedure – Cambridge City Council

Neighbour Disputes/Nuisance

This covers a whole range of issues for example:

- neighbours disputing about boundaries
- dogs barking
- noise
- persistent loud music
- children being disruptive, abusive or loud
- inconsiderate neighbours, harassment

The contractor shall investigate a complaint of a neighbour dispute or
nuisance within 5 to 10 working days depending on the nature of the
complaint. Where physical violence is involved the contractor shall
investigate within 48 hours, involving the appropriate authorities.

The contractor shall record all complaints initiated by tenants whether received by telephone, in writing, or at the reception desk.

The contractor shall investigate all complaints by:

- visiting the party or parties concerned
- recording the actual complaint
- resolving the complaint by either warning letters, mediation or serving a Notice Seeking Possession (NSP)
- involving Environmental Health Officers where necessary, and getting them to carry out enforcement action.

Harassment

This covers racial, sexual or political harassment or based on tenants' disabilities and/or age.

Racial harassment cases shall be referred to the client or an authorised officer selected by the client who will deal with this. All harassment cases shall be investigated within 2 working days.

The investigating officer shall observe the needs of the victim, ensuring that an interpreter is present if needed. A woman should be interviewed by a female member of staff if specially requested.

The investigating officer shall record all details, including details of the harassment, the history of the incident or incidents, time, date, the perpetrators and their location, witnesses present etc. He/she shall also record the victim's preferences and ensure that there is a support network available for the safety and security of the victim.

The investigating officer shall follow the guidelines laid down by Cambridge City Council for cases of harassment and ensure that the perpetrators are dealt with (see Appendix 4). Regular statistical monitoring must take place and be reported to the client.

4.9 Conclusion

Having laid out an overall strategy towards neighbour disputes, we now move on to consider in detail the two main types of techniques which landlords will need to employ within that strategy, namely mediation (Chapters 5 and 6) and legal approaches (Chapter 7).

Chapter 5
The Mediation Process

Mediation techniques involve taking active steps to help and empower neighbours to reach a solution to their dispute for themselves rather than having measures imposed by a court or other agency.

Neighbour disputes are not all capable of resolution. At the moment disputants come into contact with a mediation service, they are not suddenly transformed into constructive negotiators who value give and take on each side. There is a great deal of fear and anxiety to get through. In some cases, complainants who expect or desire decisive action from their landlord have first to accept that more conciliatory methods are worth exploring. But the results of existing dispute resolution services suggest that taking a conciliatory approach, listening actively, helping disputants clarify exactly what issues are involved and providing an impartial, empathetic ear from the beginning does have a positive impact on disputes and disputants.

The roles of staff involved in mediation are:

- to seek information;

- explore options;

- where possible, to turn a two sided fight between disputants into a three–way search for a resolution (De Bono, 1986);

- to facilitate movement towards a solution, not to impose a settlement.

Although neighbour dispute services vary in approach, their methods can be generalised into a series of stages.

5.1 Stage 1: Defining The Problems With The 'First Party'

Someone involved in a dispute tells the mediation service what is happening because she or he wants a solution or, at least, a chance to tell their story.

- An open, empathetic approach is taken to the 'first party' (the person who delivers their story first). The assurance of confidentiality and a friendly, warm invitation to speak builds trust and confidence, particularly when people fear an escalation of the dispute.

- By using active listening, reflecting back what has been heard, and encouraging clarification of the time–scale and sequence of events and other details, dispute service staff are able to build up a picture of the situation and agree a version of events with the first party which will form the initial record of the dispute.

- It is often helpful to visit the first party at home to get a first hand view of the situation.

- Once the facts as presented by the first party have been established, the issues will become clearer and although many disputants find it difficult to prioritise issues, staff can assist in making a preliminary assessment of the most pressing parts of the problem.

- Generally, mediation services try to avoid disputants settling into positions – 'I just want those kids to respect me!', or 'He's got to pay for the damage, that's all!' – and concentrate on facts and issues. They try to establish what has happened and how that can be changed rather than recording global statements of need.

5.2 Stage 2: Discussing The Options With The First Party And Deciding On A Course Of Action

Once a clear view of the facts and issues is established with the first party, dispute service staff explain how the service works, and what the options are. These might include:

- a monitoring period to check the situation;

- a direct contact between the first party and counterpart without an intermediary;

- a visit by the service to the second party to collect information;

- the appointment of mediators who will visit both sides and seek to find a mutually agreeable solution;

- shuttle diplomacy between the two sides;

- a mediation meeting between all concerned facilitated by an impartial third party;

- a more formal process of complaint, warning or judgement aimed at the second party;

- a referral to another agency or section;

- a decision by the first party to proceed no further.

Options are realistically framed, time scales explained and the first party can then choose willingly, without coercion, but also in full knowledge of the likely consequences of each course of action. Decisions made at this stage are not irreversible and as the dispute or the attitudes of disputants change, other courses of action may be more appropriate than those originally chosen.

5.3   Stage 3: Contacting The Second Party

Almost always there is a tremendous contrast between the expected image built up by the first party and the second party as they actually appear on first contact. That is not to say that there is deliberate deception going on, just that people's views of one another are conditioned by their emotions and the positions they adopt.

For an effective resolution to be achieved, even if the disputants themselves do not come together, it is invaluable to get both sides of the story. One of the strengths of a neighbour dispute service is that it provides the second parties in disputes, many of whom have particular needs of their own, with the chance to state their cases. Dealing with them in an even handed manner can lead to much improved landlord–tenant relations. If, for example, members of an isolated group with special needs, such as single parents, young single people or ethnic minorities are being regularly complained about, they too will have access to justice. Thus, this approach can aid a landlord's implementation of an equal opportunities policy.

Strenuous efforts should therefore be made to gain consent from the first party for the mediation service to visit the other people involved. Dispute service staff need to explain that they will:

- treat all information disclosed by the first party as absolutely confidential unless there is any specific information which she or he wants conveyed to the other side;

- describe their reasons for contacting the second party in non–confrontational terms, explaining that they are 'seeking information about a situation that has come to their attention' rather than 'coming to check up on a problem' or 'lodge a complaint';

- ascertain the possibility of reaching a settlement more effectively if they speak to both sides;

- point out the limitations of effective action if they do not speak to both sides (for example, that a warning may make the situation worse).

Once contact is made with the second party, their side of the story is listened to and responded to as the first party's was. An important extra consideration, however, is an active commitment to confidentiality, resisting all temptation to relay the attitudes or information disclosed by the first party.

5.4 Stage 4: Exchange And Working Towards Agreement

The exchange stage in dispute resolution is often the most exasperating, as it includes much confrontation, reversion to the past and often a refusal to negotiate. Without it, however, there will be no real resolution. The resolution process, including exchange, is facilitated by an impartial mediator who suggests a structure and guidelines, which are negotiated and agreed by the disputants. Ground rules apply whether the disputants are all together in a room – in a mediation session – or whether shuttle diplomacy is taking place, with mediator acting both as intermediary and message carrier.

Ground rules keep the confrontation within acceptable limits:

• People are not expected to be all sweetness and light, but they are expected to focus primarily on working towards agreements rather than proving their counterparts wrong, or heaping abuse upon them.

• Participants who constantly break the rules will be warned, and ultimately declared unfit to continue.

Even though it may take time to acknowledge it, there is usually some common factual ground in both versions of a situation. The mediator's role is:

• to help the disputants identify common factual ground;

• to recognise conciliatory gestures;

• to bring the two parties towards a mutual definition of the problems and issues.

Getting the parties themselves to agree at least on what version of facts they will negotiate is a major step towards agreement.

Once issues are identified and agreed upon, disputants are encouraged to identify what can be done, and to negotiate and reach agreement on each item.

• At this stage the mediator also helps to establish what cannot be achieved and to encourage full consideration of factors which will affect the chances of successful resolution.

• Disputants themselves take ultimate responsibility for suggestions and agreements which they are happy with, and committed to.

• Dispute services aim to produce processes and agreements which are fair, and are seen to be so.

• Agreements should be workable – specific, practical and easy to monitor.

If agreement is reached, all that is left to do is to congratulate the disputants, seek some feedback if appropriate, and create a framework for future contact or follow–up as required. Checking informally on the status of agreements and the well–being of the parties in the future continues the good relationship the mediation service has built up, and also provides information with which to evaluate the effectiveness of the process and resolution.

5.5 Positive Effects Of Mediation

It is important to realise that mediation is not a straightforward sequence of interventions with a predictable outcome. Neighbour dispute services contacted during the Salford University research said that only a minority of cases involved a mediation meeting of all parties – other methods such as shuttle diplomacy were used more often. Mediation is a style of intervention, characterised by skilful, impartial facilitation by a third party, which has an inbuilt momentum towards settlement from the moment the complainant comes in contact with the process.

Mediation is based on an idea of justice not blame and is therefore constructive, promoting the value of agreement. The inbuilt momentum of such services towards settlement can cause disputants to resolve conflicts themselves and can impart greater understanding of differences between people in the local community. There are many practical advantages which derive from this:

•   It is specialised – staffed by specially trained people who can deal with the complexities of disputes, and will achieve more effective 'clear–up' rates than general complaints procedures.

•   It does not necessarily require a written complaint from the first party.

•   It offers a structured process which has safeguards but is conducted informally in language which neighbours can understand and is flexible.

•   It provides a chance to take the heat out of conflicts and is extremely effective at collecting information which is significant rather than dramatic.

•   It is able to counterbalance imbalances of power if they are not too great.

•   It aims to achieve realistic and sustainable solutions.

•   It is relatively speedy.

- It yields high levels of satisfaction from users.

- It does not remove the right to take other action, such as legal action, subsequently.

- It can deflate unreasonable claims and promote the value of agreement.

- It can deal with a variety of issues, and often heated and complex disputes.

- It improves the capacity of neighbours to deal with future disputes themselves.

What little research there is in the UK on neighbour dispute mediation indicates that clients do benefit from their contact with a mediation service, whether or not their dispute is ultimately resolved. Disputants surveyed in one study were either generally satisfied, or very satisfied with the service, particularly the atmosphere of acceptance, the capacity of staff to listen well, and the mediators' ability to deal with conflict (OPUS, 1989).

Figure 4 illustrates the benefits to disputants of resolving a dispute through mediation. At its most effective, mediation will have a positive influence on the local community as disputants become more tolerant of, and have a more positive attitude towards, resolving differences with neighbours.

Figure 4   The Mediation Process Working Successfully

The Dispute
The origins of the mediation

Feelings

- I feel threatened and *discounted* by my neighbour's behaviour ▶
- It triggers all my anxieties about the context ▶

Perceptions

- I *label* and depersonalise my neighbour ▶
- My picture of my neighbour is distorted ▶

Behaviour

- I react in relation to my distorted picture of my neighbour ▶
- My actions maintain the dispute, despite my wish to end it ▶

The Process
The experience of the mediation

- I feel listened to and understood, ie *validated* by the Centre's staff, the mediators and my neighbour ▶
- I feel less threatened and more in control of my feelings ▶

- I recognise my neighbour as a 'real person' – a fellow human being ▶
- I recognise that my neighbour also wishes to be 'neighbourly' ▶

- I see that the way we have both behaved has made matters worse ▶
- I look for new ways of relating to my neighbour ▶

The Outcomes
After the mediation session

- I feel better about life and about the local community ▶
- I am not so irritated by the minor nuisances of living close to my neighbour ▶

- I see my neighbour as an individual with his/her own needs and problems ▶
- I make allowances ▶

- I approach my neighbour, as he or she is, when I need to ▶
- We try to find ways of working out problems ▶

Source : Grubb Institute, 1990

To illustrate the nature of mediation in neighbour disputes we now describe three cases of mediation, one which went through all the above stages, and two which broke off.

....

Case Study: Mediation Successfully Completed

Mr O came to the mediation service to complain that his neighbours were 'making his life hell'. He had recently been diagnosed by his doctor as claustrophobic and put this down to a history of nuisance from his neighbours including loud piano music, children playing in the street outside his window, doors banging, verbal abuse, threats of physical abuse and actual damage to his property. He was clearly distressed and would only speak with the intake person in the general reception area, as he wanted to be near the exit in case his claustrophobic anxiety grew too severe. He was extremely angry and listed a history of complaints and conflict going back several years.

The intake person checked through the various points he had made, reflected back what the main issues were, and then explained how the mediation service could proceed. It was emphasised that they would have to speak to the 'other side', but would be tactful and that nothing Mr O had said would be relayed to his neighbours. The mediation service could not tell the neighbours what to do, nor would they take sides. The first step, it was explained, was for two mediators to visit Mr O in his home, introduce themselves and talk to him about the situation and what he wanted to do about it. Visibly more relaxed than when he came in Mr O agreed to the visit, but was highly sceptical about the possibilities of a negotiated agreement. He doubted whether Mr and Mrs S (the neighbours) would even talk to the mediators.

Two mediators were allocated to the case, and visited Mr O, who went over much of his story, and also, after a while, began to reveal some details of his personal life, which had not been happy in the last seven or eight years particularly since his wife had left him three years previously. He agreed to the mediators' suggestion that they make an appointment to visit Mr and Mrs S.

Ten days later, after having written to Mr and Mrs S, the mediators visited them and spoke to Mrs S and her son. Initially there was a considerable amount of hostility, and they wanted to know what Mr O had said. Once the mediators explained that they were impartial, had worked on many similar cases and achieved some success, and wanted to hear what Mrs S had to say, she began to relate a quite different version of events from Mr O. There had been scuffles, verbal exchanges, loud television noise from Mr O and some damage done to plants in the family's garden. Her son played the piano, but they had made every effort to reduce the noise transmitted through the wall, putting an acoustic baffle between the piano and the wall at their own cost, and encouraging the boy not to practice when Mr O's favourite TV programmes were on. Mrs S did not think she could negotiate with Mr O as he had 'become impossible since his wife left him' and would react with a stream of abuse to the 'slightest incident'. She was certainly not going to stop her son behaving like a normal, healthy nine year old. The mediators asked whether Mrs S could see an end to the dispute. She said she could not, so they tried to persuade her that maybe mediation might at least give each side the chance to talk face to face in a controlled environment, and that it was better than 'continuing hostilities indefinitely'. She declined to give a definite answer, saying she would consult her husband.

Two days later Mrs S phoned the service to say that she did not want to come to mediation. Mr O had agreed to come however, and when Mrs S heard this, she was very surprised and agreed to talk to her husband again. The next day Mr S phoned, and mediation was described carefully to him, particularly the ground rules, and the impartiality of the mediators. He agreed to 'give it a try'.

Mr and Mrs S and their son and Mr O came to a mediation session five weeks after Mr O had initially visited the service. The ground rules and procedure were explained. Mr O would speak first, then the S family, then a dialogue would be started. First each party had 'uninterrupted time', and attempts to retaliate, object or challenge what was being said were controlled calmly and assertively by the mediators, pointing out that there would be a chance for exchange soon. Half an hour later, many allegations had been made and there were some disputed facts. The mediators sought to clarify these and to gain agreement from both sides on what the main issues and problems were.

Every time the parties were asked to concentrate on how to remedy the situation they took up very inflexible positions – 'Just stop playing the piano altogether' from Mr O and 'Why don't you just move away? You're so miserable here!' from Mr and Mrs S. To try and take the heat out of the situation, and discuss new strategies the mediators suggested a break for tea about one hour in.

By the time the mediation reconvened 15 minutes later the neighbours had started talking directly to one another, having spoken mostly through the mediators up until then. They began to negotiate times when young Dean S could play the piano without interrupting Mr O's favourite programmes on TV. This was not easy, but with the mediators' help they went through a variety of options and eventually decided that he would practice early in the evening, when he first came home from school, and also between 8.30 and 9.00 in the evening. Mr O agreed not to turn his TV up too loud. They agreed to speak to one another if any other noise disturbed them too much, and to do it in a reasonable way within a day of any incident, so that feelings did not have a chance to build up. Clearly the process of actually getting angry face to face without losing control, or, for that matter losing face, had helped them see that they did have things in common – the desire for a peaceful life, to enjoy their own pleasures and be able to communicate without fighting. Two hours after beginning they left together in the S family's car, and when followed up a month later were still much happier, without any incidents or disturbances to report.

When discussing the case afterwards, the mediators agreed that they had been surprised at the initial levels of anger. However, once the neighbours had started to try to understand why they felt the way they did, forget the past and focus on the future, and negotiate directly and frankly, the mediators had been confident that agreement on the main issues could be reached. Their impartiality and conflict management skills had created a constructive atmosphere, and the neighbours realised they could both get something positive out of a difficult situation.

....

....

Case Study : Mediation not Completed (1)

Mr and Mrs W lived next door to Mr and Mrs K in a block of flats on a council estate. Mr and Mrs K complained to the local estate office, then to the Environmental Health Department about noise from loud music in the flat next door. A warning notice was served on Mr and Mrs W. When this did not result in any change in the noise, an abusive exchange took place between Mrs W and Mrs K. The husbands then got involved and a brief fight ensued. Mr and Mrs W called the police who referred the dispute to the local mediation scheme. Both sides were visited by mediation scheme staff to collect information and try to work towards reconciliation. Both parties agreed to attend mediation but the day before the mediation session was to be held Mr and Mrs K dropped out because they feared escalation and reprisal. Another noise warning notice was issued and an uneasy truce was maintained. However Mr and Mrs K were looking for alternative accommodation.

In this case there was a history of escalation (notice served, abuse, violence, police called) prior to mediation being considered. The mediators felt they had increased understanding on both sides, allowing a 'cease fire' to be maintained, but that they needed more time to break down layers of bad feeling and suspicion. If mediation had been available at the beginning of the dispute there would have been more chance of resolution.

....

....

Case Study : Mediation not Completed (2)

Mr R lived in a ground floor flat of a housing association house, below Mr B and Ms E. Mr B turned his freezer off over night and it leaked into the groundfloor flat. Repairs were carried out by the housing association, but they claimed payment of the bill from Mr B. He insisted that not all the damage was done by the freezer as the ceiling and walls were already in a bad state and therefore he was not prepared to pay the whole bill. Mr R insisted that he should not contribute. The Housing Association did not see this as a routine repair and required payment in full; they agreed to abide by the outcome of mediation. Mr R, Mr B and Ms E all attended, but could not find a formula for an agreement which suited them as neither party was prepared to compromise. In addition, other issues of complaint were brought up.

Mr R withdrew and took the matter to the small claims court where he was awarded full payment against Mr B including costs. In this case each party wanted to use the mediation process as a way of promoting their own stance. The constant recycling of old issues demonstrated a history of bad feeling which had not been previously addressed and encouraged each to seek a punitive solution. It is unlikely in this case that their resistance to compromise could be broken down without lengthy preliminary work on both sides. An arbitration may have provided a more appropriate formal framework for this case.

....

Chapter 6
Existing Mediation Practice

This chapter summarises existing mediation practice with which local authorities – particularly housing departments – and housing associations have had some involvement. It also considers the development process, from the identification of need, to the start–up of a service. Twenty five local authorities and nine housing associations, all of which had expressed an interest in mediation to Mediation UK, or were known by the researcher to be interested, were contacted. Sixteen local authorities from this sample have either adopted some form of mediation practice, or had a major part to play in the development, and in many cases, the setting up, of an independent local mediation service. No housing associations contacted during this research had yet progressed as far along the mediation route, but examples are included of some current and proposed uses of mediation by housing associations.

6.1   Why Use Mediation?

Though not all the twenty five landlords contacted were fully committed to adopting a fresh approach to neighbour disputes, or considered that they had the resources to use mediation themselves, all but one of those surveyed thought that the use of a specialised service, including mediation, for neighbour disputes, was a good idea. The first set of reasons in favour of mediation are largely a product of the failures of existing procedures:

• Existing practices seem to have little effect on a growing problem.

• A great deal of officers' time is spent on neighbour disputes with little hope of success. For example, a survey of area housing officers and senior managers in one housing department estimated that 642 person hours per week were being spent on neighbour disputes, at a cost of £3,682 per week (Communicated by the Sheffield–based Mediation Service, MESH).

- Officers do not have the time to give cases which merit long term attention, the time they deserve.

- Dispute handlers experience stress which current practices do little to alleviate.

- Feedback from tenants indicates that they are unhappy with current practices:

    –One Tenant Participation and Consultation Sub–Committee indicated that they believed the current procedures were characterised by poor liaison between departments, unclear complaints procedures, unavailability of local staff, insensitive handling of complaints and perceived lack of commitment.

    –In one London borough there had been more petitions to the housing committee concerning neighbour disputes than any other subject.

- Existing measures fail to deal with the root causes of disputes, to handle the multiplicity of issues or to provide long–term remedies.

- Legal remedies are right for certain cases but inappropriate for many others. They are expensive, unpredictable in terms of outcome, and can often make disputes worse before they get better, if they ever do.

- Neighbour disputes can escalate into serious disturbances and existing practices can often only come into play when a serious incident has occurred.

- The unwillingness of social landlords to commit resources to neighbour disputes is seen by residents as devaluing the status of their complaint. This impression is exacerbated by a sense of being 'bounced around' departments, none of whom seem interested in constructive action.

There were also quality–driven reasons given for exploring the mediation option:

- as part of a general customer care initiative;

- as a cost–effective option which does provide successful outcomes;

- as part of the aim to produce better tenant/landlord relations;

- to improve/capitalise on tenant participation and consultation;

- to enhance the skills and confidence of officers and other front–line staff, thereby reducing stress levels.

There have also been attempts to assess need more scientifically:

- Dudley Metropolitan Borough Council have commissioned a series of polls which have shown a significant increase in the proportion of tenants who believe that neighbour disputes are getting more frequent and more serious.

- Existing tenants' forums, joint tenant/landlord working parties or sub committees, or multi–departmental or multi–agency bodies have been specially assembled to collect information about current services and other options, including mediation. This approach has been taken by the London Borough of Greenwich and by Luton and Cambridge City Councils.

- The Housing Customer Services Division of the London Borough of Hackney is considering commissioning a feasibility study to assess the problem and the possibility of setting up a mediation service locally. The proposed feasibility study would include interviews with officers and tenants, assessment of the suitability of cases for mediation and examining existing dispute case files.

- North Housing Association balloted its tenants about 'beefing up' tenancy agreements, and this method could also be used to gain feedback on other procedures, including mediation.

Faced by this overwhelming evidence of the need for a fresh approach to neighbour disputes, 16 of the 25 authorities contacted had decided to explore the possibility of incorporating mediation into their work. Almost all of these were considering independent mediation services, rather than in–house arrangements. The main reasons in favour of an independent, rather than in–house, service are:

- Officers and mediators are clearly seen as impartial and not representatives of the landlord.

- The responsibilities of officers acting on behalf of a landlord preclude officers playing the role of independent arbiter. If an independent mediation service is developed officers are not put in a position where they have a conflict of interests and loyalties.

- All residents of mixed tenure areas including local authority, housing association and private sector tenants and owner–occupiers are able to use the service.

- It is seen as more representative of, and responsive to, the community.

- It is possible (though not easy) to attract funding from a variety of statutory and charitable sources.

- One organisation, for example the housing authority, will not have to bear the full cost of setting up and running the service.

The disadvantages for large social landlords are:

- possible lack of control over the service standards;

- not having sole use of the service, so having to compete with other users;

- ongoing funding may be uncertain;

- mediation may still be viewed as a peripheral activity rather than an essential, viable option;

- it may take more time establishing credibility with statutory agencies.

- it may be difficult to specify CCT contracts, especially in terms of 'success rates' (but probably no more difficult than for any other method of dispute handling).

6.2   Developing An Independent Mediation Service

What follows is a description of the process of investigation and development of an independent mediation service. Some other types of mediation initiative are discussed later in this chapter.

6.2.1 Stage 1: Initiating the process

The impetus for developing a mediation service has taken several forms, including an idea from a staff suggestion scheme, the particular interest and energy of an officer in response to previous experience or new information about mediation, and an approach from an existing service or mediation expert (see Resources Section at the end of this chapter). The seniority of the officer who initially promotes the idea does seem to have a bearing on how quickly the mediation option can gain status and momentum. Examples of this would be the Director of Housing in Bolton, the P.A. to the Director in Cambridge, and the Senior Environmental Health Officer in Middlesborough),

6.2.2 Stage 2: Collecting Information

An initial investigation should be conducted to find out:

- what mediation is and where and how more information and ideas about mediation can be obtained (See Resources Section at the end of this Chapter);

- how it works elsewhere;

- what its advantages and disadvantages are;

- the extent of local need for a service. Examples of methods of assessing need are mentioned above in 6.1.

6.2.3 Stage 3: Generating Support

Allies, supporters and interested parties will help carry the development process forward. This is done by individual lobbying, commissioning presentations from experienced practitioners, holding open meetings to discuss what mediation means and running workshops for anyone who may have an interest.

6.2.4 Stage 4: Creating a Multi–Departmental, Inter–Agency Foundation

A steering group should be set up of people who are prepared to spend time and effort taking the idea forward.

• There are a number of networks to join (see Resources Section at the end of this chapter), including local Councils for Voluntary Service, existing mediation services, Mediation UK, and newsletters published locally, which will almost certainly promote initial meetings, workshops and planning sessions.

• Within local authorities, Environmental Health, Legal Services, Social Services and Police Community Safety Units have proved to be willing allies in many areas. Interdepartmental co–operation has often been easier where there are existing multi–agency forums, networking groups, project teams, amalgamations of departments and previous experience of taking a corporate approach on particular issues.

• Support is also often forthcoming from those agencies and individuals already involved in dealing with neighbour disputes or their consequences, such as the police, advice agencies, law centres, solicitors, magistrates, doctors, probation officers and health workers.

• In existing schemes, resident and tenant participation have not always been sought at the earliest stages, but there are many examples of representatives from tenants' associations and of councillors and officers who are also local residents playing a significant role in the consultation and planning process. Such involvement does help to open up channels of communication with potential users of the service at the earliest opportunity and to ensure that the tenants' as well as the landlords' interests are strongly represented.

- To ensure that the service is able to respond to the needs of a wide spectrum of the community it is advisable to have a variety of people on the steering group who reflect the diversity of the local community in terms of gender, ethnicity, disability and sexuality and who understand and pursue equal opportunities policy and practice.

6.2.5 Stage 5: Taking A Project Development Approach – Planning And Allocating Tasks On A Step–By–Step Basis

An action plan must be developed. This should include:

- aims and objectives;

- the kind of service desired;

- who will be the mediators;

- what kind of accommodation and equipment is required;

- resourcing and funding;

- policy development;

- status of the organisation;

- constitution;

- recruitment of staff and mediators;

- promotion of the service;

- evaluative criteria.

Most of the necessary development tasks and issues are summarised in *Guide to Starting a Community Mediation Service*, Mediation UK, 1993. (See Resources Section at the end of this chapter.)

To enact the plan, employ the individuals from different sectors who have expressed interest and commitment and form sub groups to take on particular individual tasks. Once these tasks are achieved the groups can disband rather than holding endless meetings. Their energies can then be redirected into areas where progress may be slower, or where new tasks are being identified. This approach can be quite demanding, as it requires commitment, the expenditure of considerable time and energy and also careful facilitation, as different aims, values and opinions may emerge. However, it ensures that a professional, staged approach is adopted and that the energy and output of the whole steering or foundation group is at least as great as its constituent parts.

6.2.6 Recruiting Volunteers

Volunteer mediators are drawn from every walk of life and tend to represent a cross section of local communities, for example, in terms of social class and ethnic diversity. Although the majority of mediators are female, there is an increasing number of male volunteers. Some people who have previously been personally involved in neighbour disputes volunteer, either because they were helped by mediation or because they feel they would have benefitted had mediation been available.

Volunteers are recruited by increasingly professional methods. A typical publicity campaign would include the production of leaflets and press releases in local authority and community newsletters. In many cases person and job specifications can be provided to potential mediators. These should give brief details of the mediation scheme; the time commitment involved; the personal qualities required, for example the ability to deal with anger and separate oneself from disputants views; and the provision of training and support. Applicants should be interviewed and a short list drawn up by a recruitment panel. References should also be taken up before mediators are selected.

(Details of recruitment methods, examples of publicity material and specification of standard equal opportunities interviewing procedures are included in Mediation UK's *Guide to Starting a Community Mediation Service*. See Resources Section at the end of this Chapter.)

6.3 Capacity Of Existing Services

6.3.1 Numbers

It is difficult to generalise about workload, but an examination of statistics gathered by seven established community mediation schemes indicated that a total of 1,344 enquiries per annum were received by them regarding neighbour disputes, a minimum of 150 and a maximum of 270 in each scheme. This is despite the fact that the schemes were often working with a skeleton staff and very limited resources. Of these 1,344, 714 were considered suitable for mediation, and 137 reached full face–to–face mediation. (This does not mean that the 137 were the only successes – or that all mediations were successful, see 6.3.3 below).

• Maidstone, Newham and Walsall Mediation Services have calculated that 16 hours work is required from intake to completion of a full mediation.

• The 40 per cent or so of cases which involve work with one disputant or shuttle diplomacy also consume a great deal of time, between two and twelve hours, depending on whether the contact is continuing to have a positive effect on the dispute.

• Many of the cases which are not suitable for mediation also occupy co–ordinators and their assistants. Mediation services are particularly keen to ensure that they at least take their clients seriously at first contact and help them through impartial advice and information where appropriate.

Bristol Mediation considered this aspect of their work so important that they raised funds from central government for a noise counsellor, who, while encouraging the use of mediation, and getting disputants together, would also work as a counsellor with one party, particularly when they seemed to be having persistent neighbour problems (see 6.9.2 below for more details).

6.3.2 Scope And Nature Of Cases

Mediation services deal with the full range of neighbour disputes including noise, anti–social behaviour, problems with children, pets, parking, verbal abuse, boundary disputes, damage to property, litter, soiling of common areas and other issues of general nuisance. They have also had some success with low level racial and sexual harassment, and have adapted the mediation process to intervene successfully in intergroup and community disputes.

Housing organisations have used independent mediation services to a considerable extent. For example, 70 per cent of clients of Hammersmith Mediation (MEND) are council tenants or owner–occupiers who are directly referred by the local housing directorate; in Walsall the figure is about 40 per cent; in Sandwell 30 per cent; Maidstone 45 per cent and Lambeth 25 per cent. Both Hammersmith and Maidstone housing authorities are finding this service so useful and cost–effective that they are contributing significantly (Hammersmith 60 per cent and Maidstone 80 per cent) to its ongoing funding.

6.3.3 Output

In the cases deemed suitable for mediation, success can be defined in various ways, for example:

- a reduction of hostilities as one or both parties decide to take conciliatory action;

- an informal agreement reached through indirect mediation, or shuttle diplomacy;

- a general calming of the temperature, though the parties may never actually meet and discuss the situation;

- a written agreement, as the result of a face–to–face mediation session.

On the basis of the evidence available, it appears that over 50 per cent of cases achieve some measure of success, and 10 per cent go all the way through to full mediation. In a survey conducted by Maidstone Mediation, disputants were contacted 6 months after the mediation service had worked with them, and 80 per cent of first and second parties said that the service had been helpful, 60 per cent said the situation had improved, and only 5 per cent said it had worsened. These figures are in stark contrast to the views of many housing officers contacted for this study who described neighbour disputes as 'impossible', 'persistently frustrating' and 'situations that just go on and on without ever changing.'

6.4   The Cost Of A Mediation Service

Understandably, when local authorities and housing associations consider adopting new practices, one of their major concerns is cost. Before discussing the costs of existing mediation services – which show considerable variation – we propose a model of costing which concentrates on the benefits of an independent service to large social landlords, their residents and the local communities, as well as the costs.

6.4.1 Input/Output Model Of Costing

To arrive at a realistic assessment of the costs and benefits of a mediation service, we need to consider the inputs and outputs of existing methods of dealing with neighbour disputes, and compare them with those of a mediation service. Any existing procedures would contain the following tangible, practical inputs provided by the wide variety of agencies and departments which are involved with a dispute at any one time (see p.67 for one authority's costing):

- people hours – preparation, interviews, case consultations, mediations, travelling time, associated administrative work, support, training for all organisations handling neighbour disputes;

- court time and expenses;

- client time and costs – lost work output, leisure time, out of pocket expenses (research suggests that this is a significant input (Conciliation Project Unit, 1989));

- premises, equipment, maintenance, insurance, security and caretaking.

There are also the less tangible, but equally significant, human inputs:

- emotional, psychological and physical energy of dispute handlers and disputants.

Depending on the aims and objectives of existing procedures, it is expected that some or all of the following outputs will be apparent:

- a number of disputes being resolved;

- satisfaction of disputants and fulfilment for dispute handlers;

- some measure of improvement in relationships between disputants;

- an improvement in tenant/landlord relationships;

- a sense of confidence in the community about dispute handling procedures;

- a sense of money and time being well spent;

- a reduction of bitterness and tension;

- a sense of purpose and motivation for dispute handlers.

Applying these two checklists to existing procedures will indicate that the high level of input into current arrangements is not producing a commensurate level of output in any of the mentioned target areas. The views of a very large proportion of officers contacted by the authors support this opinion.

The cost of mediation should therefore be set in the context of its capacity to at least achieve significantly positive output measures. As such it will not only save time and energy but will also begin to rebuild the confidence of residents and provide large social landlords with an opportunity to regain some sense of management control of neighbour disputes.

6.4.2 Costings

There are certain essential resources for an effective independent mediation service:

- **Staff**
  A central co–ordinator must be appointed to be responsible for general administration, intake of disputes, arranging mediations, organising and supporting mediators, liaising with management, promoting the service to the community and potential referral agencies, monitoring, evaluating and developing the service.

A team of mediators is required to investigate disputes, work with disputants and assist the process of resolution, including shuttle diplomacy and face–to–face mediation. Most services see local volunteer mediators as the most satisfactory option as they are able to give a professional service, but are also perceived as having a good understanding of local conditions and problems. 'Voluntary' certainly does not mean 'amateur' as mediation services attract a broad variety of skilled, competent individuals who are committed to providing a high quality service.

- **Recruitment and Training**
  Correct, professional, equal opportunities procedures of recruitment ensure a service gets competent paid and unpaid workers, and that they know what is expected of them. Training will initially be bought in for co–ordinator and mediators in basic mediation and other associated skills and techniques. Given time, training, skills and experience, the co–ordinator or experienced mediators will be able to perform the function of trainer to the service.

- **Administration**
  Existing mediation services are not excessively bureaucratic, nor do they insist on written complaints. However they all require a diary of appointments, visitors and mediations; record of contact forms including basic details of cases, action taken and outcomes; monitoring procedures (including equal opportunities monitoring of ethnicity, disability etc.); information and publicity materials; information about other relevant and helpful agencies and individuals; financial systems including volunteer expenses claims and records, cash book and invoice file.

- **Rooms/Equipment**
  One room is the minimum requirement for operation of intake and administration, but an additional room will be required for mediation sessions. Minimum equipment is a direct telephone line, answerphone, wordprocessor or typewriter and access to a photocopier. Waiting or reception space is also useful, as is a meeting room for mediators, staff and the management committee. Ideally the location should not be directly identified with a particular agency. However, compromises often have to be made to keep overhead costs down and there are many examples of services which have been able to overcome the suggestion that they might be biased or controlled by their host agency, by the way they handle disputants, reassuring clients of their impartiality.

6.4.3 A Realistic Budget

Mediation services are currently being run in this country for as little as
£3,500 a year, and as much as £45,000. These figures are a little misleading
as, at the lower end of the financial scale, much of the service is dependent on
time given free by experienced, competent professionals who volunteer as
co–ordinators, mediators, administrators or development workers. Figure 5
shows a reasonable annual budget of £30,000 for the first year, compiled by
comparing 14 budgets of existing or proposed services. On this budget it
should be possible to deal with in the region of 500 enquiries producing about
250 cases suitable for mediation.

Figure 5   A Typical Budget for An Independent Mediation Service

	£
Co–ordinator	18,000
Training	2,000
Office costs	5,000
Volunteer expenses	2,000
Publicity	1,000
Set–up	2,000
Total	**30,000**

Notes

a. Office costs include rent, insurance, equipment rental, stationery.

b. Set–up costs are unpredictable, but may include furnishings, equipment,
promotional events, launch, consultancy fees.

c. In certain parts of the country some expenses may be higher e.g. staffing costs in Central London would include London Weighting of c£2,000.

d. Staffing is limited to one full–time co–ordinator, with around 12 volunteers. As the case–load increases and the service becomes established locally, a half–time administrator would almost certainly be needed and would add around £6,000 to the annual budget.

e. Salaries include National Insurance.

6.4.4 Creative Resourcing

The *Guide to Starting a Community Mediation Service* (Mediation UK, 1993) gives plenty of tips about charitable and statutory sources currently prepared to fund mediation services but competition for funds is great and success rare. There have been some creative responses to the funding problems:

*   **Cross–sector or inter agency funding**
    Both community and family mediation schemes have been funded by a combination of interested agencies who see the benefits in terms of their own quality of service, and the saving of time for their officers who would otherwise have to handle neighbour disputes. Cross–sector working at the early stages of development helps establish the credibility to raise local authority funds from specific committees such as Housing, Social Services, Environmental Health or Public Protection, Community Development or Police. Cross sector lobbying and influence has also resulted in core funding from Policy and Resources committees and more generalist local authority sources. The amounts required are really not large in the light of the potential positive output measures.

*   **Secondment, placement or other direct involvement by existing staff**
    In the development stages and even in the setting up of pilot schemes, housing, environmental health and other staff have been authorised to spend time working on behalf of the mediation service. There have also been instances of skills being imported free of charge to conduct recruitment, evaluation and administration on professional lines. No examples of secondment to co–ordinator posts have been found, possibly because of the potential conflict of interests or associations with bias. There may still be room for such an arrangement as such a secondment

would enable an officer to get hands–on experience and training which she or he could subsequently pass on to other staff.

- **Secondment from industry**
  One or two services have sought to recruit people for particular development and support tasks from commerce and industry. This may well be an option worth exploring further, particularly with retraining programmes or schemes for recently retired people who have the relevant skills.

- **Free use of resources**
  Premises, equipment, materials, mediation rooms and other resources have been made available to services either free of charge or at very reduced cost.

- **Sponsorship**
  This requires some time to negotiate but there are examples of sponsorship of publicity materials, office costs and equipment.

- **Use of Volunteers**
  Some services have tapped into the considerable interest in mediation which exists in our communities and discovered people who are prepared to fill crucial roles such as co–ordinator, administrator or even trainer. The disadvantages of being so dependent on volunteers is that they sometimes have other priorities or do not stay because they see the job as a stepping stone to another paid post. For this reason it may sometimes be difficult to plan the workload or deal with urgent cases when the only resource is volunteers.

6.5   Working Practices

There is variety in working practices of mediation services but the following generalisations and guidelines can be made:

- At 'intake' most services record basic details of clients' situation, name, address, age and a brief history of the dispute.

- If a client is seen to have special needs then some services allocate a particular worker who has skills or experience in this area.

- The practice of matching mediators and other staff with clients by ethnicity, age and other variables is also used by some dispute services, although there is little research to suggest conclusively that matching actually works.

- Once 'intake' has been completed, some services insist that the same people (staff or volunteers) continue with the case, right up to mediation if necessary.

- Others, to use advanced skills as economically and efficiently as possible, use one group of people, usually less experienced or trainee mediators, as 'case developers' or 'interviewers' working with the clients up until the mediation, where experienced trained mediators take over.

- Mediators often work in pairs, particularly pairs which demonstrate the impartiality of a service (for example a male/female pair with family mediation). Disputes often involve clashes of lifestyle, values and culture and some dispute services choose to allocate people who reflect those differences but model cooperative working rather than conflict (for example, black and white mediators where there is black/white conflict). In addition, co–working provides a built–in opportunity for mutual support and feedback.

- Solo–working is also used extensively and many mediators feel they can be more in control of the process working on their own. Economics also play a significant part in determining working practices in schemes with paid mediators.

- A neighbour dispute service should strive to ensure that the people involved in the service represent a cross section of the local community and that high standards of equal opportunities practice and policy are achieved.

- Mediation services are flexible and resourceful. Walsall Mediation, for example, have recently developed a three–point plan which they present to disputants, who can opt for face–to–face mediation, shuttle diplomacy or a negotiated statement of intent, agreed by both sides without them ever meeting and monitored by the mediators for a fixed period.

- In general, when paid or non–paid staff and mediators are recruited from minority, specialist or special needs groups this has a rapid positive impact on that potential client group and the credibility of the service.

- Mediation services do have a reasonably successful track–record in dealing with disputes where groups such as ethnic minorities or victims of domestic violence have previously had little power. However, when basic human or social rights are transgressed or where conflicts escalate into persistent harassment or abuse, then more formal processes should take over.

6.6　Intake Criteria

Some mediation services have experienced the 'dumping' on them of particularly difficult cases with which no other agency has managed to achieve success. Others have had the reverse problem of 'over–loading' caused by estate staff opting out of sensible early treatment of minor disputes and referring all cases to the mediation service just because it exists.

Also some potential clients arrive with no real understanding of what the mediation service has to offer. It is the service's responsibility to educate the general public and referral agencies about its work and also to develop greater clarity in the criteria they and referral agencies use for intake. Decisions should be made on each case on its merits. The following factors are some of those which existing services should consider:

- the history and dynamics of the conflict;
- the possibility of physical threat;
- the complexity of issues;
- the nature of the relationship between disputants;
- the intensity of feeling;
- willingness to participate in the resolution of the dispute;
- the existence of problems of communication, mutual understanding and perceptions;
- the capacity of the disputants to resolve the issues in dispute;
- the specialised nature of the issues at stake (is expert knowledge required?);
- whether or not other agencies are involved;
- whether legal action is pending, or in process.

Housing authorities have been referring disputes to mediation services which have the following characteristics:

- low levels of anger and physical or verbal intimidation;
- no serious breaches of tenancy agreements;
- allegation and counter allegation;
- insufficient evidence for other landlord action;
- facts which are unsubstantiated;
- disputants who appear susceptible to reason;
- disputes involving mixed residency, for example tenants and owner–occupiers;
- room for improvement in tenant relationship;
- disputants who are not initially prepared to have face–to–face contact with their counterpart.

Mediation service staff contacted during this research felt that these criteria formed a reasonable basis for deciding upon cases which should be referred to them. However, there is a need for the mediation services, as well as agencies referring cases to them, to give serious consideration to developing appropriate criteria for making intake decisions.

The use of mediation is not appropriate if:

- there is an extreme power imbalance between parties;
- there is repeated abuse or behaviour which breaches basic codes of behaviour;
- either side continues to insist on a punitive judgement to apply external rules or sanctions;
- either side is not competent or willing to participate in the process, or consider settlement;
- continued intervention, even of the most subtle and facilitatory style, may either affect the well–being of one or both of the disputants or have an inflammatory effect on the dispute.

6.7   Resistance To Mediation

Resistance to mediation is likely to be encountered and can manifest itself in a variety of forms both in terms of the views and behaviour of disputants and the opinions of tenants, housing officers and other statutory and voluntary bodies. Some of the kinds of resistance that can be expected are as follows:

From disputants

* psychological and emotional investment in maintaining fixed positions and perceptions, due to the intensity of the dispute;

* persistent attachment to the win/lose mentality;

* behavioral and emotional fluctuations which emerge as people arc asked to face up to problems and deal directly with them;

* difficulty perceiving what is 'in it for them' as mediators clearly do not take sides;

* fear of direct contact with their adversary;

* attachment to the status quo and fear of change, no matter how unsatisfactory the situation may seem from outside.

From disputants and other agencies:

* lack of understanding of what mediation is (a confusion with meditation still occurs!) and suspicion associated with its novelty;

* a sense that it may be a soft option which offers perpetrators of harassment and nuisance an easy way out;

* a view that it is a kind of quasi–judicial process, or 'justice on the cheap' (Volpe and Bahn, 1987).

Mediation services need to deal constructively with such resistance. Using conventional mediation wisdom – i.e. explore, identify interests and issues, define the problem and seek positive options to achieve constructive outcomes – services and mediators will discover that by exploring these fears and levels of resistance, they will grow to understand the interests and issues involved and develop positive strategies for overcoming or, at least, modifying this understandable resistance.

6.8   Staff Training In Mediation

During the course of this research, officers and staff at all levels have acknowledged that handling neighbour disputes is a difficult process. To be effective, dispute handlers need patience, good communication skills and relationships, common sense, an understanding of equal opportunities issues, the ability to remain calm under pressure, questioning skills and the capacity to make decisions and plan a course of action. As one senior manager said 'these are not cheap skills' and not all staff dealing with neighbour disputes possess these qualities and skills in abundance. As we said earlier, good training is needed for all types of dispute handling.

For mediation work, the particular skills and characteristics required are:

- the ability to remain impartial and demonstrate this to disputants;
- an awareness of ones own prejudices, reactions to conflict and ability to deal with other people's emotions;
- the capacity to gain and maintain trust;
- an understanding of the nature of conflict and conflict behaviour;
- active listening skills;
- facilitation skills;
- the ability to manage conflict and assist others in negotiating;
- sensitivity to other people's feelings, values and opinions;
- a willingness to learn.

All mediation training courses are based around these foundation skills and characteristics, and would typically contain the following elements:

- what is mediation? – theory and context, aims and values of constructive conflict management;
- building self–awareness and confidence – our reactions to conflict, understanding and handling our prejudices, impartiality;
- core skills – active listening, questioning skills, gaining trust, empathy not sympathy;
- the mediation process – how does it work;
- creating the right atmosphere;
- contact with the first party;
- contact with the second party;
- exchange either through shuttle diplomacy or mediation;
- clarifying facts, defining issues, interests and options;
- encouraging negotiation and working towards agreements;

- dealing with difficult behaviour, managing conflict;
- making agreements and follow–up;
- working for a mediation service – administrative requirements, support and ongoing training.

Several housing authorities and associations have sent their officers on either complete mediation courses, or introductory workshops or seminars. There have also been examples of training staff in–house.

Cambridge City Council gave all its estate managers basic mediation training, which they found extremely useful, although residents found it difficult to separate the managers from their landlord role. Because they have hands–on experience of the benefits of the mediation approach, the council is now playing the lead role in setting up an independent service in Cambridge and the surrounding districts which will be a free service to the general public.

Middlesborough's new independent mediation service is one of several that plans to use its co–ordinator, once trained, as trainer for the local authority's housing and environmental health officers. This is a creative method of increasing the potential output of the mediation service and improving the capacity of front–line officers to handle disputes.

Perhaps the most comprehensive staff training initiative in mediation which has been developed so far is the Dudley scheme. The Neighbourhood Conciliation Officer has developed a five half–day package for housing officers. This has one session each on the roles of the police, legal action and environmental health officers' in dealing with neighbour disputes and two half days on the skills and techniques associated with visiting the first and second parties. This training was developed as a direct product of hands–on experience, and is now part of regular housing officer training. In addition, the scheme has piloted 120 hours of study, taken as an adult education course and accredited by the Black Country Access Federation called the 'Good Neighbours

Mediation Course'. Through a combination of classroom and practical learning and home study, participants have been able to study and practice dispute resolution. The pilot course was attended by concierges, receptionists and clerks many of whom subsequently agreed to form a mediators' network for the resolution of disputes in their area.

Details of trainers and training packs on mediation can be obtained from Mediation UK (See Resources Section at the end of this chapter)

6.9   Other Mediation Initiatives

6.9.1 In–House Initiatives

There have been several examples of in–house initiatives in the area of mediation. These include Bolton's Mediation Service which has been driven by the Housing Department, although it has not been entirely funded by the local authority; and the appointment in Dudley and proposed appointment in Greenwich of local authority officers who provide mediation style approaches to neighbour disputes.

Bolton's Mediation Service

Bolton's Mediation Service is, in effect, an independent service but it has been driven by the Bolton Metro Housing Department from the beginning as part of its commitment to a comprehensive customer care service. Recruitment of volunteers was conducted by the Project Co–ordinator who is supported by an Assistant Director of Housing. The premises are located in an estate office. Although some potential clients in the early days confused the service with the housing authority, for example expecting to have to pay rent arrears before they could use the service, it is functioning as an independent service. Voluntary mediators have been carefully recruited and trained to be impartial, and are now seen as such by the local community. The service does not only take referrals from the Housing Department.

....

Dudley's Neighbourhood Conciliation Officer

In July 1991 Dudley Metropolitan Borough Council appointed an officer who describes himself as 'semi–independent' who is responsible to the Senior Estates Officer. His job purpose is 'to provide a neighbourhood mediation service where tenants will be able to discuss and resolve disputes with their neighbours, and to train Estates Office Staff in dealing with neighbour disputes, and to contribute to Departmental Policy.' He is essentially a co–ordinator and mediator rolled into one and had handled 120 disputes up until February 1993. He believes that his involvement in disputes has given them a degree of status which can itself do much to smooth complainants' ruffled feelings. The vast majority of cases have been resolved using shuttle diplomacy. The training element of his work was discussed in the previous section. Throughout his employment the officer has been researching the nature of disputes, the time spent dealing with them through mediation and other methods, and this information will not only be useful for local policy makers, but also for developments in this field in general.

....

....

Proposals for Nuisance Officers in the London Borough of Greenwich

As yet these appointments have not been made, but it was the intention of the London Borough of Greenwich to appoint several officers to perform a monitoring, investigating, advisory and counselling role with local residents, co–ordinate the joint responses of other agencies and liaise between council departments, particularly housing and environmental health. They would deal with a variety of nuisances including harassment and neighbour disputes. Although mediation was not in their specific remit, the principle of effective intake and on–the–spot investigation with both disputants could be seen as moves towards a mediation style approach. A representative of Greenwich Housing Rights cited three advantages to the proposal, which has not yet been agreed:

> 'Most radically, it gives a single officer, equipped with
> multidisciplinary training, the ability and authority to take a corporate
> overview. Secondly the officer would be specialist and though a
> housing officer, would not be faced with difficult prioritisation
> decisions over different areas of work. Thirdly, from the point of view

of tenants, a single named officer could be seen to be taking
responsibility for the problem and could be held accountable.'

··

6.9.2 Specialist Noise Counselling Services

As we saw, noise is by far the most common cause of neighbour disputes. It
has therefore been a natural development for Environmental Health
Departments to have specialist noise officers. However, up to now it has been
very rare for mediation services to specialise in this way. The only case the
authors have found is in Bristol.

··

The Bristol Noise Counselling Service

The Bristol Mediation Noise Counselling Service was set up in 1992 to
implement an independent Noise Counselling Service working
co–operatively with Bristol City's Health and Environmental Services in
order to provide an efficient and coherent response to domestic noise
complaints and find satisfactory resolution to them. By directly addressing the
social, personal and interpersonal aspects present in some domestic noise
complaints the Noise Counselling Service aims to counsel clients and to
support them in the following appropriate courses of action in order to
improve their situation in an effective manner.

Referrals are taken from Health and Environmental Officers in two sorts of
circumstances: where no statutory noise nuisance can be substantiated but the
noise problem persists, and where support may be needed during the
investigative stage in a case.

Cases have involved the following issues:

> neighbour dispute or feud; prejudice (race, gender, students, sexuality
> etc); hearing sensitivity due to mental or physical condition e.g.
> cancer, tinnitus, M.S., depression; special requirements of work life
> e.g. shift working; attempting to use EHO to get rehoused; family
> problems.

In almost all cases the Counsellor works with both parties, bringing them together as mediator to create agreements where appropriate and helping to develop alternative self–supportive strategies where not.

6.9.3 Housing Associations – The Partnership Approach

In the field of family mediation for divorcing and separating couples there are a number of examples of fruitful partnerships in running a service, including service contracts. This research has discovered that some housing associations are keen on working with existing mediation services on a similar basis for mediation in neighbour disputes. One such example is the London and Quadrant Housing Trust, who refer cases to Southwark Mediation, though they still have only limited links of any formal kind. A manual for staff from London and Quadrant Housing Trust also mentions that 'mediation should always be the first step', although it does not envisage its own officers acting as mediators. Merseyside Improved Houses indicated, in a report to Directors in November 1992, that as well as officers of the association attempting to act as mediators in disputes, there is some interest in 'participating in the development of such a (mediation scheme)' rather than instigating such a project alone. The most developed example of service agreements or retainers by housing associations with mediation services appears to be in Walsall. This may set an interesting precedent which other associations will wish to follow. It may be more difficult for housing associations with properties spread over a wide geographical area to use retainers to one particular mediation service; they may wish to work on a 'payment by case' basis.

Partnership between a Housing Association and a Mediation Scheme

A provisional agreement has been reached between Walsall Mediation and Caldmore Area Housing Association for the latter to pay a retainer of between £5,000 and £7,000 a year. In return Walsall Mediation undertakes to:

- take on all neighbour disputes referred by the association whatever the root cause or presenting problem;

- provide on site basic mediation awareness training to Housing Officers;

- provide detailed statistics on the service for the year (reviewed with Housing Officers every four months);

- provide leaflets to tenants and promote the service to tenants groups;

- provide statements of full costs to enable staff to evaluate the mediation service;

- provide special reports to key staff who deal with special projects, e.g. housing of the elderly/infirm/mentally ill/young people etc;

- examine tenancy agreements in order to review and update them;

6.10 Evaluation

Evaluation of mediation in the UK is in its infancy. In this guide, we have merely been able to give examples of good practice and a method of estimating the value of mediation through an input/output model. This section gives some suggestions of factors to consider in the evaluation of what some describe as the science, and others the art of mediation:

Organisational factors

- success at reaching agreements;

- nature of agreements;

- compliance with agreements;

- stability of agreements over time;

- cost of agreements;

- efficiency with which agreement is reached, including speed, but not sacrificing efficiency for speed;

- access to justice and fairness as perceived by disputants.

Personal Factors for Customers

- effect on others' needs and well–being;

- relational development, including communication;

- satisfaction with outcome and process of mediation;

- psychological and emotional effects;

- perceptions of the mediators' competence;

- reduction of conflict and stress;

- procedural and substantive fairness (Menzel 1992).

6.11 Conclusion

We can conclude then that, to be successful, Neighbour Dispute Services need to have the following characteristics:

- They are seen as fair and independent particularly by users and potential users but also by referral agencies, statutory bodies and community groups.

- They are well publicised and promoted:

    –establishing a high profile with a wide variety of potential clients, referral agencies and support agencies;

    –creating understanding of the nature and benefits of dispute resolution methods amongst managers and front–line staff dealing with complaints and enquiries from the general public (for example the Police and housing organisation staff);

    –producing good quality information and publicity materials.

- They are accessible:

-with conveniently placed offices, which are pleasant to be in and
with good physical access;

-with efficient but informal intake procedures;

-able to receive personal calls, phone and mail enquiries and act on
them quickly;

-able to institute resolution procedures speedily.

- They are broad based, with staff, volunteers and management committee
or supervisors who represent a broad range of people from the community
and are able to gain the trust of clients.

- They have a solid funding/resource base.

- They have at least one key full time worker, a person who acts as
'gatekeeper', receiving and deciding action on enquiries and promoting
and co–ordinating the service.

- They offer professional standards of service, support, training and
development for staff (paid or volunteer).

- They take equal opportunities seriously, monitoring and targeting the
characteristics of customers and potential client groups.

- They provide a high quality service:

-being seen to be effective by clients, funders, paid staff and
volunteers;

-setting realistic targets and monitoring how they are met;

-having effective recording, monitoring and evaluation procedures;

-addressing issues of competence and performance of paid and
volunteer staff within a constructive framework.

Resources Section

An up–to–date list of currently operational mediation services and local authorities who have shown an interest in or actually instituted some form of mediation practice, including those surveyed in this research, can be obtained from:

Mediation UK,
82a Gloucester Road,
Bishopston,
Bristol BS7 8BN
Telephone 0272 241234
Fax 0272 441387
Contact Marian Liebmann – Director

This is the national organisation of community mediation, which offers advice on setting up schemes and can put you in touch with trainers and generally assist on mediation matters.

Conflict Management Plus,
47 Cranleigh Road,
London N15 3AB
Telephone 081 802 3525
Contact John Crawley – Director

Provides comprehensive advice, consultancy and training for work with neighbour disputes.

Chapter 7
When Persuasion, Threats
And Mediation Fail

As we have seen in Chapter 3, a common reaction of landlords when persuasion, threats and attempts at mediation fail, is to walk away from the problem telling the tenants 'to sort it out themselves'. This is in spite of the fact that landlords (and local authorities in their other capacities) do have administrative and legal powers to act in serious cases. These powers include the voluntary transfer of one of the parties (see 3.2) and the use of statutory nuisance proceedings, injunctions and eviction. In this Chapter, we discuss the legal position in England and Wales; specific legal differences in Northern Ireland and Scotland are dealt with in Legal Appendices 2 and 3.

7.1 Environmental And Public Health Legislation – Nuisance

Powers to deal with certain kinds of unneighbourly behaviour are found in the Environmental Protection Act 1990. Under this, statutory nuisance proceedings can be taken to deal with matters which are prejudicial to physical health or a nuisance. These powers are available to local authority landlords in their capacity as environmental health authorities; housing associations would have to depend upon the services of the environmental health officer to deal with any statutory nuisances arising in their properties.

···

Types of Statutory Nuisance within the Environmental Protection Act 1990

- Certain types of smoke, which includes soot, ash and grit (though usually not domestic smoke or smoke from industrial or trade premises which are separately controlled under the Clean Air legislation) – the provision (section 79(1)(b)) could cover, however, certain 'unneighbourly' bonfires;

- Fumes and gases (S79(1)(c));

- Accumulations or deposits (S79(1)(e));

- Any animal kept in such a place or manner as to be prejudicial to health, etc (S79(1)(f));

- Noise emitted from premises (S79(1)(f)).

···

The types of statutory nuisances which are most relevant within the neighbour dispute context are accumulations and deposits, animals and noise.

- A person may offend against a neighbour by dumping rubbish or excreta on land adjoining that of the victim. Or a person may accumulate rotting matter on their own premises so that they become prejudicial to the health of those around. The smell from animals may certainly constitute a nuisance.

- Noise, a frequent cause of neighbour disputes, may amount to a nuisance if it can be shown to have an adverse effect on the use and enjoyment of property and to have a general relevance to health. In this context the law appears to accept that any noise which creates undue interference with comfort and convenience can be a statutory nuisance.

A local authority may take summary proceedings to abate statutory nuisances (actual, apprehended or likely to recur) in its area under S 80 of the 1990 Environmental Protection Act.

- Authorities must first serve an 'abatement notice' on the person responsible for the nuisance (or on the owner or occupier of the premises concerned, if the perpetrator cannot be found or where the nuisance is anticipated). The notice must require the abatement of the nuisance and may require preventive or remedial action.

- Where a nuisance arises from a noisy party, the organisers can all be 'persons responsible', and an Environmental Health Officer called to deal with such a situation may be able to serve the notice directly on such persons. As an alternative, where organisers cannot be identified by name, notices may be addressed to 'the occupier' of the premises.

- An abatement notice is subject to a right of appeal to the magistrates. Where this right is not exercised, a subsequent failure to comply with the requirements and prohibitions of a notice, without reasonable excuse, constitutes an offence.

- Since 1st October 1992 the maximum fine on summary conviction has been £5000.

- An appeal against an abatement notice suspends it until the court has decided the matter, but a local authority in some cases can prevent this suspension by including a statement in the notice that it is not to be suspended because the nuisance to which it relates is injurious to health.

- Failure to comply with an abatement notice also entitles authorities to take any necessary remedial action. For this purpose, their rights of entry in residential premises are subject to 24 hours notice to the occupier but officers can circumvent this restriction by obtaining a warrant to enter from a justice of the peace.

- In some cases the person served with the notice will be able to rely on a defence that he/she used 'the best practicable means' to prevent or counteract the nuisance. This is generally restricted to situations where the nuisance arises on industrial, trade or business premises, and so is not relevant to residential neighbour disputes. More of a problem in noise nuisance cases is the requirement that the noise must be emitted from 'premises'. 'Premises' is defined to include land, but it is still debatable whether a public open place would be classified as 'premises' (Tromans, 1990) (See, however, below legal appendix LA1.3 on the proposals to deal with some street wise nuisances in the Noise and Statutory Nuisance Bill 1993).

There may be cases where Environmental Health Officers need to enter premises to deal with noise but are refused admission. If Environmental

Health Officers are to obtain a warrant of entry, a justice of the peace needs to be convinced that reasonable grounds for entry exist and that one of a number of specific situations exists, for example,

• that admission has been refused or refusal is anticipated, or

• that an emergency exists and that there is reasonable ground for entry into the premises for the purpose for which entry is required.

'Emergencies' are defined by Schedule 3 paragraph 2 (7) of the Environmental Protection Act 1990 as situations where it is reasonably believed there are circumstances likely to endanger life or health and entry is necessary to ascertain whether those circumstances exist, or to find their cause and take remedial action. It is believed an 'emergency' could exist in a noise nuisance situation where the effect of noise is widespread and/or where the health of persons is being prejudiced because they are losing sleep (DOE 1992c).

....

Cases of the Use of Statutory Nuisance Powers

Mr Bostock, a hermit, developed a mania for collecting putrescible material – meat, fish and vegetable matter – in his home. The material attracted rats, mice and other vermin and became a breeding ground for flies. Council officials cleared the material on a number of occasions but Mr Bostock collected more. In due course statutory nuisance proceedings were taken against him, the authority relying on S 92 of the Public Health Act 1936, the predecessor of S 79 of the 1990 Act, and the common law authority of *Attorney–General v Tod Heatley*, 1897. Mr Bostock refused to obey the orders despite prosecution. Ultimately the authority sought an injunction against him in the county court under S 22 of the County Court Act 1984 (see now S 3 of the Courts and Legal Services Act 1990), the validity of which was upheld by the Court of Appeal. When Mr Bostock ignored the injunction he was imprisoned for nine months. [*Wyre Forest DC v Bostock*, 1992]

Ms Mawdsley was a teenager who had been accommodated by Liverpool City Council Social Services Department in a care home. That home closed and Ms Mawdsley was initially reaccommodated in a hotel, then in one of the authority's flats. Neighbour disputes arose almost at once. Residents in the block of flats complained in a concerted fashion that Ms Mawdsley played loud music at all hours of the day and night. The council attempted to defuse the situation by offering Ms Mawdsley a set of headphones and further offered to set a device to limit the volume of her stereo equipment: both offers were refused. Alleging the noise was a statutory nuisance, the authority acted under S 80 of the 1990 Act to require abatement of the nuisance and when Ms Mawdsley refused to comply and technically committed an offence the authority relied on S 81(3) of the 1990 Act to take steps to abate the nuisance themselves. The authority obtained an order from the magistrates authorising their officers to enter the defendant's flat and seize the stereo equipment. [*Liverpool CC v Mawdesley*, 1992]

It is believed that equipment seized in order to abate a noise nuisance's occurrence or recurrence may be retained under a local authority's general powers to facilitate the performance of its functions under section 111 of the Local Government Act. Furthermore where a conviction for the commission of a statutory nuisance has been obtained, section 43 of the Powers of Criminal Courts Act 1973 empowers the court to make a deprivation order in respect of property lawfully seized from an offender at the time of his/her arrest, or at the time a summons in respect of the offence was issued, and which was used by the offender for the purpose of committing an offence (DoE 1992c, paras 35 and 41).

Particularly in the case of noise, offence to others can arise from what the perpetrator may well believe is his/her legitimate pursuit of pleasure, rather than any wilful anti–social behaviour. For this reason, as we have stressed throughout, it is important that landlords attempt to solve the problem by informal means before resorting to the law and, for instance, seizing equipment. Indeed the need for a staged and carefully thought through approach to such action has been stressed not only by the Ombudsman, but also by the government:

'Authorities should regard the seizure of equipment as a course of action to be used sparingly and only in those circumstances where the noise nuisance is very severe and persistent. If an authority decides to go ahead it will have to demonstrate in any case that its use of the powers in section 81 (3) was reasonable, and this would have to be judged as a question of fact in each case' (DoE 1992c para 28).

Authorities are well advised to obtain a warrant before equipment is seized.

···

Compromise on the use of statutory nuisance powers

Mr Harris was a member of the well known brass band Desford Caterpillar Band. He practised his cornet at his semi–detached house in Coventry. This, it was alleged, upset his next door neighbours and Coventry CC took noise abatement proceedings under the Environmental Protection Act 1990 banning Mr Harris from practising at home. Mr Harris appealed, supported by the Musicians' Union, and the matter finally came before the Crown Court. The court lifted the ban but restricted practising sessions to one hour a day [*Coventry CC v Harris*, 1992]

Mr Harris claimed afterwards, according to *The Times* for 10 August 1992: 'The decision establishes that making music is not a public nuisance ... We have a basic right to be allowed to practice on our instruments.'

···

7.2 How Useful Are Environmental Protection Act Proceedings In Dealing With Neighbour Disputes?

Such proceedings are irrelevant to the vast majority of disputes. Alleging someone's behaviour amounts to a statutory nuisance is to accuse that person of a crime: such a course of action should therefore only be followed where the behaviour complained of is gross and all other attempts at alternative resolution have failed. In any case the existence of a statutory nuisance has to be proved beyond reasonable doubt, and no authority should pursue such proceedings without a good body of evidence on the matter, for example, a number of documented complaints from neighbours about the behaviour and evidence from environmental health officers such as, in the case of a noise nuisance, decibel level readings taken from fixed and identified points. In all cases the precise details of the nature, source and location of an alleged nuisance are needed. It must also be remembered that because a failure to comply with an abatement notice may involve the defaulter in criminal proceedings any subsequent interviews with that person should follow Police and Criminal Evidence Act 1984 procedures.

7.3   Landlords' Possession Actions

A landlord can take possession action against offenders when they are its own tenants. The landlord may do this *either:*

- by relying on an ability to seek possession against those tenants who commit acts of **nuisance** or annoyance to neighbours;

or

- by writing **conditions into tenancy agreements** forbidding certain types of behaviour, for the breach of which conditions possession may be sought.

This latter method of proceeding raises, of course, issues as to how effective such techniques are in imposing normative behaviour on those subject to them, as well as ethical issues as to whether and when it is acceptable to adopt this method of social control. There is also the moral dilemma of imposing the sanction of eviction on a whole family, especially one with small children. Reluctance to enforce such a sanction weakens the persuasive power of threatened action.

The powers available to landlords are set out, for secure tenancies, in section 84 and Schedule 2 of the Housing Act 1985, and for assured tenancies in section 7 and Schedule 2 of the Housing Act 1988. Further general comment on possession orders can be found in the Legal Appendix at A1.4.

The general 'no nuisance' grounds in the two acts are very similar, providing, in the case of the 1988 Act, that possession may be sought where: 'the tenant or any other person residing in the dwelling house has been guilty of conduct which is a nuisance or annoyance to adjoining occupiers, or has been convicted of using the dwelling or allowing the dwelling house to be used for immoral or illegal purposes'. However, the court will also consider the interests and responsibilities of the landlord and the tenant and the wider public interest.

Two complicating factors should be noted in the use of the 'no nuisance' grounds for possession. The first is that the behaviour must relate to the property; it is not enough if it arises elsewhere. The second is that, where the offensive behaviour is that of someone living in the tenant's home, judges can be unwilling to attribute responsibility to the tenant where the offender appears to be beyond the tenant's control (Forbes, 1988, pp.64 and 301). This creates considerable difficulty, particularly in the case of children's behaviour. However, as the first of the following cases shows, this unwillingness on the part of judges is not universal.

....

Case Study: A Judge's Willingness to Attribute Responsibility to a Tenant for their Child's Behaviour

A couple were tenants of a council house and their 16 year old son was responsible for a series of racial attacks and abuse against a neighbouring Pakistani family. For two years the victims had been subject to abuse, such as the woman of the house being called a 'Pakistani bitch' and being followed by the perpetrator while he chanted racial insults and spat on her. The Pakistani family's son, now aged 8, had been beaten up by the perpetrator. The teenage boy by way of response claimed he was a victim of lies, and that the two daughters of his neighbour, aged 10 and 11, had stared at him 'in a funny way'. The County Court Judge concluded that a possession order should be made effective from 30th November 1992. He did this even though he concluded the teenage boy was beyond his parents' control. He concluded of the family: 'The quicker they are removed from the area the better for all concerned'. The house in question was let under a tenancy containing specific clauses banning the racial harassment of neighbours. It is thought this was the first case of this type in Birmingham. *(Independent,* 27 Oct 1992)

....

....

Case Study: Nuisance away from the Premises and Cautious Legal Advice

Location
Rehabilitated flat in quiet residential area on the edge of Nottingham City on the fringes of an established 'red light district'.

Problem
A known prostitute was living in a housing association property, soliciting on the street outside a children's nursery during daytime hours as well as evenings. Nuisance was caused by kerb–crawlers approaching both the prostitute and the local female population. Regular callers came to the flat at all hours and discarded used condoms in the gardens and street.

The housing association, as the landlord, were accused by both residents and the police of inactivity and even condoning the actions of the prostitute by not evicting her. Staff of the housing association followed the classic approach to anti–social behaviour of confronting the tenant, liaising with the police, requesting 'diaries' of incidents from local residents and instructing solicitors. Initially the legal advice was that the housing association could not take action against the tenancy under the 'nuisance' or 'immoral use' tenancy clauses. The nuisance was not occurring on the premises, but in the street and despite convictions for soliciting no link could be made to the flat and there was no evidence of more than one prostitute using the flat.

Neither the police nor the local residents would accept this legal advice.

Only after the police agreed to provide witness statements from arrested kerb–crawlers and under cover policemen who were 'invited' into the flat were the legal advisers prepared to recommend action for possession. Counsel's opinion sought at this time said that the Association had a 50% chance of winning a possession case. Further informal advice reduced the odds if the tenant were to be represented by a local active and effective legal practice.

Outcome
The tenant eventually abandoned the flat before the court date arrived and subsequently moved in with a vulnerable neighbour (also a tenant of the same housing association) and continued her trade. The tenant of this property subsequently moved out voluntarily.

Conclusion
The case caused problems over a two year period and the housing association's 'ability' to manage was called into question by local residents, local councillors, the Housing Corporation, the police and initially the local MP. The fact remained however that legal advice had been taken and despite the fact that in this instance the housing association could call upon two police officers, two local residents and two staff members as witnesses in the possession case, Counsel's opinion still only gave a 50% chance of success. The possibility of failure of the action was too disastrous to contemplate.

....

The use of 'no nuisance' grounds of possession is also often problematic because of the specific wording in the 1985 and 1988 Acts. Although it seems clear that the nuisance complained of can be one that affects more than just those who are contiguous to the offender's property (see *Cobstone Investments Ltd v Maxim*, 1985), it does not follow that all those who live in a neighbourhood are neighbours; a degree of proximity is required. But, there is flexibility in that it appears that the 'nuisance' in question need not amount to an actionable nuisance at common law, that is, for a landlord to take action against a tenant it does not have to be proved that another tenant of the same landlord could have successfully brought an action in tort for nuisance on the basis of the behaviour about which the complaint is made.

The final characterisation of an activity as a 'nuisance' is a rationalisation after the event by a judge of a set of circumstances in which a whole range of issues will have been taken into account in coming to a decision; for example:

- Was there a substantial interference with the use and enjoyment of the complainant's property by the offender's activity?

- Was that interference 'sensible' (ie capable of being measured in some way)?

- Was the interference the result of a continuing state of affairs?

- What was the nature of the locality in which the nuisance occurred?

- Was there any malice on the part of the offender towards the complainant? (Hughes, 1992).

To the question of 'what constitutes a nuisance?', the answer is often, therefore, the infuriating response, 'it all depends'. 'Annoyance' is a wider term than 'nuisance'. For annoying behaviour to constitute a nuisance it must be such as would annoy a reasonable neighbour (see *Tod–Heatly v Benham*, 1889). Examples of types of behaviour that are annoying and a nuisance include:

- keeping disorderly dogs that run loose on estates and foul streets;

- regularly holding noisy or disorderly parties;

- committing acts of racial harassment such as shouting obscenities at a neighbour who is a member of an ethnic minority;

- allowing children to 'run riot';

- using premises for prostitution or for patent displays of immorality such as sexual exhibition, though cohabitation by unmarried couples is not an 'annoyance' for the purposes of defining what constitutes annoying behaviour (see *Yates v Morris,* 1950 and *Hodson v Jones,* 1951, and *Heglibiston Establishment v Heyman,* 1977).

Rather than using the 'no nuisance' ground of possession, some landlords prefer to insert specific clauses in tenancy agreements prohibiting types of conduct which, if they then occur, constitute breaches of condition in respect of which possession may be sought (see Ground 1 of Schedule 2 of the 1985 Act and Ground 12 of Schedule 2 of the 1988 Act). A survey conducted by the National Consumer Council (1976) found that 94 per cent of the 318 English housing authorities questioned had a 'tenant shall not be a nuisance to neighbours' clause in their tenancy agreement.

....

Case Study: Using Possession Proceedings to Deal with Persistent Breaches of a Tenancy Agreement

A housing association took a firm approach to a neighbour dispute in which their attempts to achieve resolution by discussing the problem and urging a change in behaviour had failed. The housing association did not take lightly the decision to go to court to enforce their tenancy agreement and had never before evicted a tenant. The case also illustrates the possibilities and value of working with several agencies and local residents as well as the need to be sensitive to the problems of the family concerned. However, the housing association did not appear to make as much effort as it could have done to help Ms L to modify her behaviour to make it more acceptable to her efforts.

The housing association had no internal policy document on how to handle neighbour complaints apart from a general complaints handling policy document, but a standard procedure was normally followed. When a complaint was received there was usually an internal meeting between the area housing manager, the relevant housing assistant and another housing assistant. A plan of action was then agreed upon. The housing assistant visited the complainant and the accused to establish the facts of the case. The severity of the case determined the response made but the first response was always to give the person the benefit of the doubt. Staff of the housing association stated that the majority of cases could then be resolved by the housing assistant. If this was not possible the area housing manager became more involved, usually through writing letters but in more serious cases through personal visits. More senior management rarely got involved but the regional manager would make principal officers and the management committee aware of the case, especially if there was the possibility that it might lead to legal action.

Complaints were first received about Ms L in January and February 1988, largely concerned with noise levels and troublesome children. In the same period the police had been called out by the neighbours. The housing assistant wrote Ms L a 'gentle' letter asking people in the house to be quieter. At this time the housing association was giving Ms L the benefit of the doubt; she was a young person and many of the complainants were elderly; they thought it might 'only have been a clash of lifestyles'. In March 1988 a housing assistant visited Ms L about the disturbances her children were causing but Ms L denied all charges. After this visit a stronger letter was sent, again from the housing assistant, which ended by bringing the tenancy agreement to her notice.

No more complaints were received until July 1989. From July 1989 to September 1989 there were 15 incidents reported to the police about Ms L. Housing Association C had received 12 complaints from various sources in the same period (many about the same incidents the police had been called to). After receiving five complaints Housing Association C asked complainants to put their grievances in writing.

Following the receipt of a letter from Housing Association C strongly restating the terms of the tenancy agreement about nuisance and overcrowding and stating that Housing Association C viewed the situation very seriously, Ms L contacted Housing Association C and discussed the complaints and the overcrowding of her house. She also stated that threats had been made against her.

Two weeks after this a councillor received 15 letters of complaint about Ms L and the case seemed to escalate from that point onwards. Complaints had come from other tenants of Housing Association C, council tenants and owner occupiers. Indeed 24 separate households had complained to Housing Association C about Ms L and a group complaint on behalf of local residents was made. The complainants had also gone to a local Community Health and Information Service. The complaints were about a variety of issues but were fundamentally concerned with noise and disorderly behaviour. It was found that Ms L's home was overcrowded and that alongside Ms L and her three children lived another woman and her three children. In addition several men were often seen to use the house for the children were sometimes left unsupervised. Other complaints concerned the use of the house as a place where car thieves met and dumped their stolen cars; two people had been arrested from the house in connection with stolen cars.

From the outset Housing Association C worked closely with a number of different agencies interested in the case. At the initial stage in 1988 Housing Association C involved social services who had in fact had previous dealings with Ms L. Social services were largely concerned with the welfare of the children whom they believed might be at risk. As a result they knew of Ms L when Housing Association C contacted them and in the end helped the Housing Association when they wanted to seek possession of the property. The police were heavily involved in the case, having been called out by complainants on numerous occasions. They also produced a report for Housing Association C which was used against Ms L in court.

Housing Association C also had contact with the local councillor. He had received 15 letters of complaint about Ms L and whilst holding one of his surgeries some 100 people had pointed out to him the problems at Ms L's property. He then took the complaint to Housing Association C and the police and asked for all concerned parties to hold a meeting and discuss what could be done. The councillor played a coordinating role in bringing the various agencies together.

A meeting was held between the association, the police, eight residents and the councillor. From this a number of measures were agreed upon; Housing Association C would be willing to take Ms L to court to seek possession, the police were going to make their presence felt and the residents were willing to give evidence in court.

As a result of this meeting Housing Association C took legal action against Ms L (only the second notice of seeking possession (NOSP) Housing Association C had served concerning a housing management problem; all others had been against squatters), they therefore now placed the complaints in the hands of their solicitors. Housing Association C's solicitors liaised closely with other agencies largely to seek clarification of various issues concerning the case. The solicitors also conducted interviews with four complainants who were willing to give evidence in court. Ms L contacted Housing Association C to find out about the NOSP, Housing Association C advised her to go to the Citizens' Advice Bureau or to get legal advice. They told her that she would not be rehoused by them, so she must declare herself potentially homeless. Ms L agreed that she had brought this situation upon herself. At this stage Housing Association C contacted the local housing aid centre and informed them of the case and of the fact that they were going to seek possession.

The case did go to court, after one month's deferral because Ms L had failed to seek legal aid. (If the case went to court without Ms L seeking legal aid, there was the risk of the local authority declaring her intentionally homeless.) At the second hearing neither Ms L nor her legal representative turned up and the judge awarded possession to Housing Association C. After this Ms L bowed to pressure and moved out of the property of her own accord without being evicted.

....

Landlords do not have carte blanche to include any restrictions they wish in their tenancy agreements. The power to include particular provisions in an authority's tenancy agreement exists within the context of the general powers of a landlord to manage housing, and therefore clauses should only be included that are germane to housing management. It would not appear possible therefore to have a general clause prohibiting a particular type of conduct on the part of a tenant against *any* person *anywhere* within, say, an authority's district. However, some local authority landlords have introduced clauses governing conduct on their estates, particularly in relation to racial harassment. Similar clauses have also been introduced as covenants on Right to Buy sales, particularly in the case of leasehold sales (See Legal Appendix A1.3).

The Housing Services Advisory Group (HSAG, 1977) stated as the purpose of tenancy agreements that they should

'achieve, on the one hand, the quiet and peaceful enjoyment of the property by the tenant and, on the other hand, the efficient management and administration of the local authority's housing stock, with due regard being paid to the rights and interests of all other tenants, neighbouring owners and occupiers... [There] should be regulation to govern the rights, duties and conduct of the tenant as well as obligations on the part of the landlord...'

The Types of Clauses Controlling Offensive Behaviour that are Commonly Encountered in Local Authority Secure Tenancy Agreements (Forbes, 1988, pp57–60):

- clauses prohibiting nuisance or annoyance supplementing the 'no nuisance' ground for possession so as to make it clear that the tenant will be liable for the conduct of visitors, visiting members of his/her family, lodgers and sub–tenants, or to extend the ambit of liability for nuisances committed against those who are not neighbours, or to prohibit offensive behaviour outside the context of occupation of the home, for example to prohibit the harassment of a neighbour's children on their way to school;

- clauses specifically prohibiting racial harassment;

- clauses prohibiting nuisances by dogs, for example to prevent dogs from running loose on estates, and to control their defecation and urination – such a clause may take the form of a prohibition on the keeping of dogs without the landlord's consent which is then given subject to requirements that the tenant abides by a code of conduct in regard to keeping the dog;

- clauses making tenants specifically responsible for the offensive conduct of others;

- clauses to control nuisance or harassment arising from parties;

- clauses to prohibit damage to council property or its defacement etc by graffiti;

- clauses enabling the local authority to withdraw the use of facilities from those guilty of offensive behaviour, eg garages, laundries, parking spaces etc;

- in relation to common parts, eg in blocks of flats, clauses restricting their use.

Some local authorities have considered introducing clauses into their tenancy agreements forbidding specific types of behaviour which are found unacceptable by the majority of tenants or by the landlord, such as racial harassment or dealing in drugs. But apart from racial harassment such clauses have very rarely been introduced.

....

London Borough of Hackney's Anti Racial Harassment Clause in its Tenancy Agreement

'The tenant must not do or permit to be done on the premises or any part of the estate or immediate neighbourhood any acts which in the opinion of the Council may be or become a nuisance or annoyance to any persons including harassment, racial or otherwise. Racial harassment includes any action which interferes with the peace and comfort of a member of a household or interferes with services reasonably required by such a member for the enjoyment of their right to occupy their property because of that member's (or another household's) racial or national origin'.

....

....

Two Examples of Social Landlords who Decided Against Introducing Tenancy Agreement Clauses Forbidding Specific Types of Behaviour

Bolton Council considered introducing a clause into their tenancy agreement banning drugs dealing, following pressure from members who wanted to see action to tackle a growing drugs problem and from the Tenants' Federation which wanted a specific clause, forbidding drug dealing, to be inserted in the tenancy agreement. It was eventually decided that no advantage would be gained from such a clause. Existing clauses forbidding running a business or causing a disturbance (such as would result from groups of people loitering close to premises from which drugs could be obtained) could be used against dealers and in some cases against users.

Salford City Council also decided against introducing such a clause because it was felt that it would be very difficult to prove that drug dealing was occurring, especially because witnesses to such behaviour are often intimidated by the offenders and so are unwilling to provide evidence.

....

7.4   Pitfalls In Possession Proceedings

Many landlords are reluctant to use their powers to seek possession.

One survey found that 54 per cent of local authorities did not regard eviction as a realistic sanction even as a last resort. Forty one per cent said it was a realistic sanction but most of these would only use it in very extreme cases and only if all other measures had failed. None of the authorities who had evicted tenants involved in neighbour disputes for breach of the tenancy agreement had made more than an average of one eviction a year (Grant, 1987).

There are several reasons why landlords are reluctant to bring actions for eviction:

• The legal sections of local authorities, often acutely conscious of budgetary constraints, are frequently unwilling to take court action where they feel they do not have a good chance of winning.

• There is frequently weak co–ordination between local authority housing and legal departments with a lack of support and guidance given to housing officers by lawyers. Smaller housing associations may lack in–house legal expertise.

• There is also an understandable desire on the part of social landlords and their officers not to be seen to be 'worsted' in court by a tenant against whom they take unsuccessful action.

• Legal sections will want to feel sure that the evidence the landlord wishes to rely on is reliable. Nuisance actions are also not easily won and judges in the County Court may require a great deal of proof before granting the remedy sought – proof that may have to be put forward in a highly formal way, such as, in the case of a noise nuisance, a 'diary' detailing the matter complained of, the type of noise, its dates and time of occurrence, its duration and quality. The complainant may not be able or willing to supply such evidence or have it corroborated.

- District judges, who hear most possession actions in the County Court can often regard neighbour disputes as 'six of one and half a dozen of the other' and so are unsympathetic to the landlord's attempts to gain possession.

- Fear of reprisals may cause victims and witnesses to be unwilling to act as witnesses.

- Witnesses may need assistance, for example in the form of child–minding and transport, to get to the court. Explanations may also need to be given to employers about time being taken from work.

- The law tends to reinforce the reluctance of landlords to be involved. For an 'annoyance' to pass the threshold of becoming a legal nuisance, the matter complained of must clearly have gone beyond the bounds of 'give and take', 'live and let live'.

- A tendency for courts to award suspended possession orders makes the weapon of possession ineffective and further inhibits witnesses and victims.

- The feeling that the problem is merely pushed to another address.

- The feeling by local authorities that the 1985 Housing Act Part III (homeless persons) makes the sanction ineffective for many families, although they may, of course, be deemed intentionally homeless.

Sometimes housing organisations try to evict the offender on grounds other than the alleged nuisance caused to a fellow resident if this appears to provide a greater chance of successful court action. For example, in a case in the Salford survey involving drug dealing in a neighbour's flat, the complainant said she had been told by her housing association that they were trying to evict the offender for rent arrears; however nothing had been achieved two years later. The Local Ombudsman (Laws, 1990) encourages the use of both grounds, pointing out that a more limited approach could lead to delay if, for example, the tenant began to pay off arrears.

Where it is decided to take possession proceedings it must also be determined who is to take the lead, eg, in the case of a local authority, the housing, legal or environmental health department. Delay is dangerous, because memories of events fade, while a neighbour dispute bad enough to warrant taking possession proceedings is likely to escalate. Yet it also has to be remembered that the handling and timetabling of a case once it is commenced is entirely at the discretion of the court and its officials – and procedures vary widely from court to court. A court hearing may be expected within 5–8 weeks of the date of the application for a possession order being made to the court.

In the case of a secure tenancy, notice in compliance with Section 83 of the Housing Act 1985 must have been served on the tenant (Section 7 of the Housing Act 1988 in the case of assured tenancies), which generally means that twenty eight days notice must have been given to the tenant.

A case can be listed directly for trial, or a pre–trial review can be ordered in which case the matter will be delayed. Further delays may be caused by orders for directions, discovery (ie disclosure) of documents, drawing up witness statements for exchange under the Courts and Legal Services Act 1990 etc. Because of the heavy workload of the courts, it can be at least a year before a possession action finally gets into court. With this lapse of time, witnesses' memories may not be reliable.

Proceedings should not be commenced unless due authority to do so has been obtained, for example, in the case of a local authority, from the housing committee. However, housing organisations may formally delegate powers to commence proceedings in such circumstances to their officers.

All the technicalities required by the law must be observed, otherwise the defendant may be able to upset the proceedings on a technical procedural issue. This matter is dealt with at greater length in the legal appendix to this guide, but it is worthwhile remembering that where there is an active law centre or specialist legal aid firm in an area to advise tenants, defendants' cases can often be ably and aggressively defended. Obviously those faced with dispossession should have access to expert advice and assistance, but involving lawyers in possession proceedings arising from a neighbour dispute can finally end the prospect of dealing with the cause of the dispute and restoring peace and harmony. Lawyers use adversary tactics which promote confrontation rather than compromise which is why the law is a 'last resort'.

7.5 Lessons From Possession Actions To Combat Racist Behaviour

The greatest scrutiny of possession actions has been in the specific context of combatting racist behaviour by tenants against ethnic minority neighbours and lessons can be learnt from these studies for more general aspects of neighbour disputes. The following issues which courts have considered as pointing to the reasonableness of making a possession order against an offending tenant have been identified (Forbes, 1988):

• there is continuing harassment;

• other victims (potential or actual) are in the area;

• harassment has occurred often over a long period;

• the harassment is serious;

• the harassment is malicious rather than merely inconsiderate;

• the harassment is clearly racially motivated;

• the victim is in a genuine state of fear;

• there are problems of housing management caused by the harassment;

• the harassment is extensive;

• past harassment has been discouraged or ended by the granting of possession orders;

• there is a warning in the tenancy agreement that harassment may lead to possession proceedings;

• the tenant has been subject to similar proceedings in the past;

• the tenant has been, or will be, offered alternative accommodation if an order is made;

• an injunction will be insufficient to prevent harassment;

- that it is the tenant who is actually being offensive as opposed to, for example, his/her children;

- that where it is family members who are being offensive the tenant is condoning their behaviour or is taking no steps to stop it, though in full knowledge of it;

- the inconvenience to the victim should he/she have to move in consequence of the offence;

- problems in rehousing victims, such as a lack of suitable alternative accommodation.

On 17 February 1993 Leicester City Council became, it is believed, the second Midlands authority to obtain a possession order against a tenant on grounds of harassing abuse and annoyance. The tenant had displayed racist literature from his home, and had abused his neighbours. The case took eight months to reach a conclusion and three court appearances, finally ending with the tenant admitting his behaviour in court. The tenant's counterclaim, that because he was of German origin, he had himself been abused by neighbours as a 'kraut', collapsed because he had no evidence to support his contention.

The following factors have been found to point to the non–reasonableness of making an order (Forbes, 1988):

- where the offending tenant is elderly or has lived in the property for a long time;

- where the victim provoked the offender or retaliated;

- where the offensive behaviour has ceased;

- where there has been quite a lapse of time since the offensive behaviour ceased;

- where possession is being sought vindictively rather than as a means of housing management and/or as a means of protecting the victim;

- where the victim has been rehoused;

- where the offender has made reparation for any loss or damage caused and has apologised;

- where the tenant did not him/herself cause the offence and took steps to try to prevent those living in his/her house from being offensive;

- where there are young children in the tenant's family and they were not responsible for the harassment.

It is quite clear that many of the above issues are relevant to any neighbour dispute. Judges in the County Court, the forum where possession issues are fought out, are also likely to consider as part of the overall reasonableness issue:

- the homelessness consequences of making an order against a tenant;

- the fact that depriving a tenant of a secure tenancy takes away from that person the valuable right to buy;

- the clear intention of the legislation in both the public and private sectors to give at least a degree of irremovability to tenants – the purpose of the legislation is to keep people in their homes.

In effect, then, a landlord going to court for possession as a result of a neighbour dispute, is by no means assured of success.

7.6 Injunctions

An injunction is a court order which prohibits a particular activity or requires someone to take action, for example to avoid a nuisance being caused. It can be granted provided the court is convinced that damages would be an inadequate remedy. Injunctions may be sought by any landlord. Some housing organisations, such as Manchester City Council, have started to use injunctions in an attempt to tackle vandalism, violence, harassment, abuse, threatening and unneighbourly behaviour, graffiti and noise.

Normally the ability to seek an injunction would be limited to the person(s) who had actually suffered from the nuisance. However, an injunction may also be sought by a landlord where it can be shown that the tenant is in breach of a tenancy condition not to indulge in particular sorts of behaviour, provided tenancy agreements are clearly and unambiguously drafted. In addition a landlord may obtain an injunction to prevent a tenant causing permanent damage to premises which have been let to him/her. (The circumstances in which an injunction may be sought are discussed in more detail in the Legal Appendix, A1.5).

- Once it is established that the tenant is in breach of a tenancy condition, the landlord may seek an injunction to restrain a breach of that condition, normally without having to prove that breach has caused damage to the landlord. In such cases the discretion of the court to refuse an injunction will be limited, for it will be quite clear that the agreement between the parties was that a particular 'thing' should not happen, or that a particular course of conduct should not be followed, and in such cases all the injunction does is to carry the parties' true intent into effect.

- An injunction can only be sought against a party to the contract. In the present context this means only the landlord and only the tenant, not for example the tenants' children or visitors, etc. However, a properly phrased tenancy condition could prohibit a tenant from permitting or inciting others to indulge in particular types of offensive behaviour.

- An injunction may be *perpetual* i.e. a final order, or *interlocutory*, which is an interim order pending the final outcome of the matter.

- Injunctions may also be classified as 'mandatory' ie those which require a positive act to be done, 'prohibiting', those which restrain unlawful activity and 'Quia timet', those which restrain the doing of some *threatened* unlawful activity.

- With an interlocutory order if the nuisance ceases no further action is taken, if it continues a perpetual injunction must be sought.

- An interlocutory order may in an emergency be obtained *ex parte*, i.e. without the defendant being given notice of the proceedings and thus having no opportunity to appear before the court, but is normally *on notice*, in which case the defendant may contest the issue.

- Where an order is sought *ex parte*, affidavit evidence from complainants, giving their names, will be essential to support the application, but witnesses do not have to go to court. Court appearances would, however, be necessary in any subsequent proceedings for a perpetual injunction.

• Injunctions granted *ex parte* will only last for a few days to 'freeze' a situation, and are normally followed by an application for a further interlocutory injunction.

• With regard to interlocutory injunctions sought on an *ex parte* basis the court must particularly be satisfied that:

    –at the final hearing there will be a serious issue to be tried;

    –the balance of convenience favours the granting of an order;

    –damages alone would be an inadequate remedy.

• Injunctions are discretionary remedies; the court must be persuaded it ought to grant an order and judges may be unwilling to grant an order they feel they cannot enforce, eg because there is no means of ensuring compliance with the order.

• Failure to comply with an injunction is contempt of court which is punishable by fine and/or imprisonment.

Manchester City Council recommends sending a copy of any injunction obtained to the police, because, though this confers no powers of arrest on the police, it may encourage them to treat seriously a further incident of offensive behaviour by the person subject to the order.

The Use of Injunctions by Manchester City Council

The experience of Manchester City Council, which started seeking injunctions in 1992 has been that they can be effective in controlling unneighbourly behaviour. When appropriate an injunction is sought against people breaking the clause in the tenancy agreement which prohibits causing a nuisance. The initiative originally came from housing management staff but received the support of tenants groups and councillors. Housing staff are aware that some judges in the County Court are reluctant to grant injunctions and have therefore been careful only to seek them when they can put forward a strong case, supported by conclusive evidence.

After nine months, sixteen injunctions had been obtained and all except two were regarded as immediately successful in stopping the offending behaviour. In other cases warning the offender that an injunction would be sought had been effective. In two cases where the offending behaviour continued despite the injunction, possession action was taken and the tenants have now been evicted. The fact that there had been a prior history of injunctions was helpful in making the case to the court for possession.

Injunctions have covered a wide variety of subjects, the most frequently occurring being noise with associated fighting and drunkenness in some cases. Other subjects include trespass by a squatter, the threat to knock down a wall in the course of a boundary dispute and driving over a green.

A Partially Successful Injunction

In one case which Manchester City Council dealt with, a court order was served on the tenant of a flat and prohibited noise and fighting, which was caused by his son who lived in the flat without the tenant's permission. The injunction was based on a new clause, inserted in the tenancy agreement a few months earlier, making tenants responsible for the behaviour of their guests. However the tenant said he could not persuade his son to leave and that he had contemplated seeking an injunction to force him to go. The Council supported the tenant in this and he got Legal Aid to sue for trespass. The son was ordered not to enter the flat but broke the order. An order for the son's arrest was issued and as a result he left the flat in order to evade arrest. In this case the Council pursued its policy of using injunctions to stop nuisance but took steps to avoid taking action against the tenant who had played the smaller part in this disturbance. They offered to rehouse the tenant away from the block of elderly people's flats if the son returns and had also previously offered to house the son but he would not accept the types of property they were able to offer him.

Local authorities may also take action to obtain injunctions in specific circumstances under their statutory powers. Where a statutory nuisance exists and the local authority concludes that its powers under the Environmental Protection Act 1990 are insufficient to deal with it by taking the case before the magistrates, they may, under Section 81(5) of the Act, seek injunctive relief in the High Court. However, the costs of High Court proceedings may be considered prohibitive and such a course of action is therefore only likely to be followed in the most extreme cases.

7.7 Combining Possession Proceedings With Those For An Injunction

Such a combination is useful where a tenant defends possession proceedings because an interlocutory injunction can still be obtained on day one of the action opening in court – and if that is sufficient to deal with the issue no further progress with the possession action need be made. It also has the advantage of giving the landlord a number of choices of how best to proceed, eg pursuing one remedy or the other, or both so that even if possession is not finally awarded the trial judge still has to deal with the request for an injunction.

The evidence the landlord has to produce to support the injunction application can be identical to that required to support the claim for possession, but it will have to be in affidavit form. It should include:

• a statement from an appropriate officer;

• statements preferably from two or more tenants affected by the behaviour complained of;

• statements from other appropriate staff scheduling the complaints.

However, such joint proceedings must be brought speedily; any delay may prejudice the grant of an injunction. The proposed order has also to be most carefully drafted for the court will not sanction an order which is incapable of being enforced. This is a particularly important issue where it is sought to restrain behaviour by people living in the house other than the tenant.

7.8   Advantages And Disadvantages Of Proceeding By Way Of Injunction

Advantages

• Injunctions are especially useful to housing management staff because they can be obtained rapidly (within 24 hours of a complaint being made in one case), and if necessary without a warning being issued.

• The aim of obtaining an injunction is to change behaviour rather than simply moving the problem to another location through a transfer or eviction.

• If the injunction succeeds in restraining the behaviour complained of, there is no need to press on with any possession proceedings.

• Where an interlocutory injunction is applied for pending the full trial, potential witnesses are protected against the offensive behaviour in question and a 'breathing space' is provided in which the landlord can check to see whether the defendant is capable of moderating his/her behaviour.

• The defendant may give an undertaking to modify behaviour pending full trial and this may be needed because the date of the trial may be some time in the future, eg because of time lags in processing the defendant's application for legal aid.

• The fact that interlocutory injunctions can be obtained on an ex parte basis on the basis of affidavit evidence helps reassure complainants who are too frightened to back up their complaints by giving evidence in court. Even though subsequent court appearances will be necessary in any proceedings for a perpetual injunction, an interlocutory injunction can give personal protection to a complainant by requiring the offender to stay away from him/her.

Disadvantages

• An interlocutory injunction is likely to be made for only a limited period of time, eg three or six months and then, if the matter is not ready for full trial, an extension will have to be sought.

- Where an injunction is sought coupled with possession proceedings, and it appears to the court that the injunction is all that is needed to restrain the behaviour in question, the court may be unwilling to grant a possession order.

- Where an injunction is breached the punishment inflicted may not be severe. Where imprisonment is imposed the term may be suspended or it may be for as little as one or two weeks.

- Speedy action is needed to seek relief by way of injunction, courts do not react well to 'stale' cases.

Local authorities have been found to be quite successful in gaining injunctions (both perpetual and interlocutory) to prevent racially harassing behaviour amounting to nuisance or annoyance. The interlocutory injunctions have often been associated with possession proceedings which can then be indefinitely adjourned once the offensive behaviour in question has ceased (Legal Action Group, 1990). Evidence from Manchester City Council supports the argument that an interlocutory injunction, especially one obtained ex parte, is a useful remedy in cases of severe and continuous racial harassment, especially cases involving assault. Manchester also recommends the remedy in cases where a tenant is damaging property, eg where major work has been commenced which could cause structural damage to a neighbouring house.

On balance, housing organisations using injunctions are hopeful that they will provide an easier, more effective way to deal with offensive behaviour and that such action will be applicable to a larger number of cases.

....

Case Study: The Use of a Variety of Legal Powers to deal with Persistant Nuisance caused to a Neighbour

The following case–study, of a neighbour nuisance complaint made to Mid Devon District Council, includes the use of the Environmental Protection Act, an injunction and a transfer in dealing with the problem.

Local authority tenants, Mr and Mrs A, had been causing noise over a period of four years by their use of a portable radio. The housing department and police had been involved in trying unsuccessfully to stop the nuisance. Eventually environmental health officers became involved. After a verbal request to turn the radio down and a standard 'noise' letter were ignored, environmental health officers served a noise abatement notice on Mr and Mrs A under the Environmental Protection Act – this had no effect. Officers visited them and set a maximum decibel level of 40 and showed them how high the volume control could be set without exceeding this level. A level of 62 decibels has since been recorded.

The officers then got a warrant of entry from magistrates and went in with the police to seize the equipment. Within half an hour the noise had resumed, Mr and Mrs A having obtained replacement equipment.

The case was taken to Exeter County Court where a temporary injunction, which ran for three months, was obtained to prevent noise nuisance on the grounds of breach of the tenancy agreement. Environmental health officers had wanted to seek an injunction under the Environmental Protection Act to pursue the matter but this would have required costly action in the High Court and the local authority solicitors did not feel competent to deal with such a case. Mr and Mrs A signed written undertakings not to exceed the maximum noise levels set by the environmental health department. There were no problems for a month and then the injunction was breached on at least three occasions.

Environmental health officers were deliberating whether to issue a letter warning of the consequences of breaking an injunction or to take the matter straight back to court. In the light of the fact that Mr and Mrs A have a family of three young children, officers were mindful of the potential effects of eviction or imprisonment. However, in the meantime, the victims of the noise nuisance had accepted the offer of a transfer from the housing department. Before the injunction expired environmental health officers met with the solicitors and decided to obtain a 12 month adjournment of the injunction. This meant that if noise nuisance was the cause of further complaints from the new neighbours within that time the Council could go back to court to seek a perpetual injunction. However, environmental health officers thought that the noise had quietened down and that the new tenants of the property adjoining Mr and Mrs A's house were more able to cope with the problem as long as noise levels did not become too excessive again.

7.9   Encouraging Witnesses To Appear In Court

Most people are unwilling to appear in court in a neighbour dispute because of fear of reprisals. There are perhaps three ways to tackle this.

First, witnesses are often more willing to appear in court in a group.

The witnesses can discuss the problem collectively, agree to appear in court as a group, and be transported to court in a mini–bus by a housing officer. It is particularly helpful if a housing officer can be the first witness in court and may be able to address the court on the nature of the tenancy agreement and the costs of dealing with the consequences of misbehaviour by tenants, for example replacing broken windows.

Second, it may be worth trying to protect the witness.

In Bethnal Green, in the London Borough of Tower Hamlets, a girl was assaulted and the windows of her council flat were broken while her father was overseas. The police charged one of her neighbours. The council issued the girl with a personal alarm and a mobile phone restricted to 999 and certain council numbers. The local council caretaker visited her regularly and the police had her recorded for a starred response to a 999 call. When she appeared in court, her neighbour pleaded guilty without a full trial.

In another case, the tenants suffered severe damage to their council flat. The flat was fitted with a security door, and a burglar alarm, and two video cameras with 48–hour tapes were mounted on adjoining buildings. Housing staff slept in the council flat on a rota basis and escorted the tenant's child to and from school. The police visited the flat every evening.

Some landlords, however, might consider such measures not to be cost effective except in relation to the most extreme cases where not only have threats been made but it is also likely they will be carried out.

Third, housing staff can act as witnesses in court.

> Some time ago there was a problem of anti–social behaviour in the Queen's Cross area of Glasgow. Residents who controlled the local community based housing association, wanted housing staff who would appear as witnesses in court. The residents asked candidates at interview what they would do if they witnessed anti–social behaviour and were threatened with reprisals. Candidates were only appointed if they answered that they were prepared to appear in court. Housing staff often appeared in court and won a number of convictions.

7.10 Conclusion

There is then a degree of consensus that using the law to evict or imprison (through an injunction) those who indulge in offensive behaviour is an action of last resort. The role of the law in this context is essentially that of dealing with those who simply will not comply with generally accepted standards of good behaviour after all managerial and administrative ways of dealing with them have failed.

Seeking possessions or injunctions are both last resort remedies, and, in the case of an eviction can only be achieved on the culmination of a long and complicated process. It is anticipated that if social landlords develop the use of mediation in the resolution of neighbour disputes there will be less need to attempt legal remedies, but they will always be needed for intractable cases. Where legal remedies are required, they need to be promptly and effectively applied.

Chapter 8
The Wider Moral Climate

It must be remembered that neighbour disputes, and the actions landlords, environmental health officers, the police and other agencies use to deal with them, take place within an ethical context.

> 'From the officers' point of view the moral mandate is as significant to their work as the legal mandate. Indeed it can be more significant, for on those occasions when the law is perceived as being discordant with popular, or individual, morality, it is morality rather than the law which takes priority.' (Hutter, p.202)

There are crucial issues about consensus or lack of consensus on what constitutes acceptable and unacceptable behaviour in neighbours and what constitutes an acceptable level of control by landlords.

A whole variety of issues may thus affect whether and how a local authority or a housing association deals with a neighbour dispute. Some have been considered; to these may be added:

- the overall policy stance of the institution – does it have a strategy of intervention in such matters;

- the personalities of the involved actors – much can depend upon the attitudes of senior officers or the influence of individual councillors/committee members;

- the resources available at any given moment in terms of personnel and skills to deal with an alleged neighbour dispute;

- the moral perception of officers of the 'rights' and 'wrongs' of any such dispute, and their views of the participants to the dispute.

'While rules are enforced by human beings, the rule and its breach will always be set in their social contexts, leading to judgements about desert or equity... Regulation in practice, mediated as it is by a bureaucracy in which people have to exercise their discretion in making judgements about their fellows, is founded upon notions of justice' (Hawkins 1984, p. 207).

Both local authorities and housing associations display a variety of responses to individual problems of offensive behaviour ranging from the very negative to the very positive.

On the negative side:

- The organisation may have no overall policy in relation to the matter.

- The organisation may have no specific clause in its tenancy agreement to deal with the issue in hand.

- Housing staff may be insufficiently trained, resourced and supported to deal with the problem.

- Legal staff may not be particularly interested in the matter or be too hard pressed to give it priority.

- The easiest way of dealing with the problem may be seen as moving the person subject to offence.

- No action may be taken because the legal outcome is too uncertain.

- The organisation/its (chief) officers may not feel ethically justified in taking action against the conduct complained of. They may feel the general climate of public opinion or sections of it do not regard the conduct as being unacceptable.

A more positive response would be that:

- The organisation has a policy on dealing with neighbour disputes.

- Staff are trained in handling disputes, with specified officers being designated to deal with problems, and a network throughout the organisation in place so that those officers can be supported by adequate legal and other professional advice.

- The organisation adopts a staged approach to dealing with complaints that cannot be informally settled, with a timetable for taking action – for example:

    (i) Reception and assessment of complaints according to set procedure.

    (ii) Mediation if relevant.

    (iii) Informal oral warning (with full details of the offensive behaviour) to the offender, if this fails:

    (iv) Formal written warning (again with full details), if this fails:

    (v) Injunction or notice of possession proceedings in due legal form, making it clear what the offence is and how this constitutes a breach of tenancy, if this fails:

    (vi) Service of injunction or notice of seeking possession.

The organisation should stand by its word and carry its threats into execution for nothing is worse than over–regulation and under–enforcement.

'Racial harassment is pernicious behaviour and all agencies should use whatever power they have to assist the process of its eradication... Legal action is not an end in itself. It is a tool which should be used in conjunction with other measures... to provide protection for the victims of racial harassment... Inaction by an authority... might be taken by the perpetrator as implying that his or her acts are publicly acceptable and condoned by those in authority. Immediately court action is taken, a perpetrator is put on the defensive... If legal action is combined effectively with work by community groups in the locality, the message conveyed to the perpetrator and others is that racial harassment is unacceptable and will not be tolerated' (Forbes, 1988, pp. 4–5).

Tightening up on approaches to neighbour disputes and particularly nuisance in rented housing is consistent with Citizens' Charter approaches to individual rights to service quality and redress and to the 'customer care' approach in the public sector. After all the desire to regulate behaviour and enforce tenancy agreements has largely originated from tenants rather than from landlords.

However neighbour disputes, involving as they do two or more opposing tenants, are more complex than the straight–forward ideas of standards and compensation which the Citizen's Charter assumes. In addition moves to regulate behaviour pose problems of the acceptability of central government, housing organisations or other tenants defining in detail what constitutes socially acceptable behaviour for the individual.

'The common good appears to collide head–on with individual rights; the local authority, as the agent of the 'common good', is perceived as the antagonist of individual freedom and consequently as a target for complaint' (Simpson and McCarthy, 1990, p.25).

In the public sector this may be seen as a move back to a more paternal style of management of public sector housing, introducing limitations which are not imposed on the majority of the population who live in private sector housing. This will become more of a problem as tenure mix in housing estates becomes more common and these conditions are imposed on some residents of an area and not on others, thus limiting their effectiveness. The point was made eloquently in the recent case, mentioned in Section 1.3, in which the London Borough of Newham tried unsuccessfully to prevent a tenant exercising the Right to Buy on the grounds that she was involved in an incident of racial harassment and that the council was

'in a better position to control what goes on against our ethnic minority tenants if we are the landlord' (*Inside Housing*, 5th February 1993, p.1).

The solution insofar as there is one, must be initially to concentrate on mediation rather than landlord–based enforcement and where legal remedies are needed, to use 'tenure neutral' approaches such as injunctions. There may also be some scope for the greater use of byelaws and the matching up of tenancy agreements with covenants on owner–occupied property.

But whatever the approach, if local authorities and housing associations are to be responsible 'social' landlords, they will have to see themselves as central to addressing the problems, uncomfortable though this may be.

Legal Appendix 1
Powers Available To Landlords And Other Agencies To Deal With Neighbour Disputes

A number of legal powers are available in a variety of situations to different agencies to promote good neighbour relations or, at least, to restrain unneighbourly behaviour.

A1.1 Other Agencies' Relevant Powers

A1.1.1 Police Powers – 'Binding Over', Breach of the Peace etc.

The police have certain powers in relation to neighbour disputes. Where, for example, violence occurs in a neighbour dispute, the police may utilise their general criminal law powers to prosecute those who injure others, or they may resort to the power of the courts to 'bind over' the participants to be of 'good behaviour'. However, it is the local authority and its environmental health officers (EHOs) who have legal responsibility for noise control. The police do not have prime responsibility and are traditionally wary of becoming involved in noise disputes unless it is to reinforce EHOs.

The power to 'bind over' is used in relation to a whole variety of public order offences. Its origins are obscure (Williams, 1967), though it is commonly associated with the Justices of the Peace Act 1361. Magistrates may order a person to enter into a recognisance, with or without sureties, to keep the peace or to be of good behaviour. Such a requirement may be imposed after a person has been arrested for a breach of the peace. Where a person fears someone will do them bodily harm, or will injure his/her child, that person may demand a 'surety of the peace' from the potential offender and the magistrates will have to bind the potential offender over if the applicant, on oath, can prove that their fear is justified. Alternatively the magistrates may bind someone over to be 'of good behaviour' which is a wider term than to 'keep the peace'. The power may be used to prevent apprehended offences and in such a case applicants need not swear that they are in fear of the person subject to the application. The power may be used where it is apprehended that a defendant will break the law (see *R. v Sandbach, ex parte Williams,* 1935), or even where that fear has passed (see *R. v Little and Dunning, ex parte Wise* 1909). In the case of a binding over to be of good behaviour, even though no criminal offence has been committed, the magistrates may exercise the power if satisfied there was conduct 'contra bonos mores' and where they have come to believe that unless restrained the defendant would repeat the conduct. 'Contra bonos mores' means conduct which the majority of contemporary persons would consider to be wrong (see *Hughes v Holley,* 1986). However, a person may only be bound over with his/her consent and the only sanction in a case of refusal is imprisonment (see *Veater v G,* 1981 and Halsbury, 1979).

Research suggests that the majority of binding over orders are made in cases where there was no specific charge, or where criminal proceedings had been discontinued (Williams, 1967). The power also has the added attraction that in a neighbour dispute the police do not have to attribute moral blame to either party. Both sides can be equally the subject of a 'binding over' order.

The Greater Manchester Police Force confirmed for this study that binding over was used both in cases where a crime such as assault had been committed and to deal with nuisance or noise incidents where no criminal charges were made. In these cases binding over is used as a last resort where an individual is causing a breach of the peace by inconsiderate rather than illegal behaviour. Staff at Manchester's Magistrates Court also said that binding over was a useful way of dealing with disputes where the offender was willing to be bound over but was probably only used a few times a year.

A further problem with the binding over power is that it can only be used against those who can be brought before the courts, for which purpose, obviously, their identities and addresses must be known. The police may request a person to give his/her name and address where they reasonably believe an offence has been committed, and section 25 of the Police and Criminal Evidence Act 1984 further empowers them to arrest where a person is suspected of having committed, or committing an offence and that person's name is unknown to the police, and they either cannot readily ascertain the name or where they reasonably doubt the truthfulness of a name given to them. Environmental Health Officers have no general power to demand names and addresses.

The police, however, have extensive common law powers to deal with or prevent breaches of the peace or public nuisances, including powers of arrest and entry to premises without warrant. A 'breach of the peace' occurs where a person suffers, or is likely to suffer, harm, or where a person's property is harmed in his/her presence, or where a person fears harm in consequence of an assault, affray, riot, unlawful assembly or disturbance. 'Public nuisance' is a wide expression apt to 'catch' a considerable diversity of deviant acts, but it certainly covers acts not permitted by law which may endanger the life, health, property or comfort of a 'class of Her Majesty's subjects'. (This somewhat arcane expression means an identified section of the community, more than just a small number of individuals). A neighbour dispute may degenerate into a breach of the peace, particularly where some of the disputants are threatening to take the law into their own hands, eg, by taking action against a noisy party. A public nuisance is only likely to occur where a whole community is badly affected by reckless or intentional unlawful activity.

The police have various other powers to deal with situations giving rise to conflicts amongst neighbours. Various statutes, including The Town Police Clauses Act 1847, The Public Order Act 1986 and The Control of Pollution Act 1974 grant powers with regard to noise, while offensive letters and phone calls may be dealt with under the Public Order Act 1986, the Criminal Law Act 1977 and the Malicious Communications Act 1984. Other legislation confers powers to control stray dogs, to take action in respect of graffiti and to regulate improperly parked and maintained vehicles.

The police themselves say that they try to deal with neighbour disputes by reaching a solution acceptable to both parties without using the courts and that they have found this to be more effective in the long term for people who must continue to live close to each other. In general the police say they try to keep their involvement in such disputes as low key as possible; they will usually talk to both parties and allow them a 'cooling off' period to consider their positions. However, if either party lodges a formal complaint against their neighbour the police are required to investigate the matter and take appropriate action.

Housing officers do not always see the activities of the police in relation to neighbour disputes in such a favourable light. Housing officers comment that the police are generally unwilling to become involved in neighbour disputes and to co–operate with local authorities when a neighbour dispute has led to criminal or civil proceedings. Housing officers say the police are often unwilling to allow evidence they have used in criminal proceedings to be further used in subsequent civil actions. Similar reluctance may be encountered on the part of the Crown Prosecution Service, and indeed there may be problems for them and the police in releasing evidence where it is held on computer under the Data Protection Act 1984.

In the Salford survey half of the tenants who called the police said they were satisfied about the outcome, a quarter felt that the police were sympathetic but did not act effectively, and a quarter said that the police were not helpful or had implied that the tenant was to blame for the dispute.

A1.1.2   Social Services

In addition to the police a number of other social agencies may be able to assist in dealing with neighbour disputes. Disruptive children may come within the powers of social services authorities under the Children Act 1989, while such authorities also have functions with regard to mentally disturbed tenants who may be causing nuisances, under the Mental Health Act 1983.

A1.1.3   Planning Authorities

Certain activities unless carried out with a grant of planning permission may amount to a breach of planning control if they constitute 'development' within the meaning of the Town and Country Planning Act 1990, ie they are building, mining, engineering or similar operations on, over, under or in relation to land, or they constitute 'material', ie marked and significant, changes of use of land. Planning control is most likely to be relevant to situations where a tenant changes the use of his/her home in a material way – for example by carrying on a business there – and this leads to nuisances for neighbours. Enforcement action may be taken against such unauthorised activity and remedial measures required. Unauthorised development is not per se criminal, but it is an offence not to comply with the requirements of an enforcement notice, and planning authorities – in the present context, district councils and London Boroughs – have powers to enter and do any works required by an enforcement notice which is ignored, and to recover their costs from the person in default.

Because particular time periods have to expire between the service of a copy of an enforcement notice and its coming into force, provision is made, where the local planning authority consider it expedient, for a 'stop notice' to be served in addition to the enforcement notice requiring cessation of the activity in question. Such a notice can come into effect within three days of being served. It is, however, possible to appeal against enforcement action and the effectiveness of planning control with regard to neighbour disputes, and its appropriateness in view of the other remedies available, must be open to a considerable degree of doubt.

A1.2 The Use of Byelaws

A further set of legal powers over neighbour disputes, is provided by the use of byelaws. District councils and London borough councils may resort to a prosecution in relevant circumstances if a byelaw has been broken. There is a general power to make byelaws under section 235 of the Local Government Act 1972.

•   Byelaws may lay down provisions for controlling the use of public open spaces and thus attempt to remove causes of friction between citizens, for example through requirements that all dogs are to be kept restrained.

•   The section 235 power allows byelaws to be made 'for the good rule and government of the whole or any part of the district or borough... and for the prevention and supervision of nuisances therein'.

•   More particularly, within the context of housing, local housing authorities may, under section 23 (1) of the Housing Act 1985, 'make byelaws for the management, use and regulation of their houses'.

>   –'House' in this context includes yards, gardens, outhouses and appurtenances belonging to the house or usually 'enjoyed with it' (see section 56 of the 1985 Act). Section 23(2) also empowers authorities to make byelaws in respect of land held for the purposes of recreation grounds and other land provided in connection with housing.

- Authorities are further required to make byelaws in respect of their 'lodging houses'.

  - These byelaws are particularly to prevent 'damage, disturbance, interruption and indecent and offensive language and behaviour and nuisances'.

  - The expression 'lodging houses' is defined by section 56 to mean 'houses not occupied as separate dwellings', which would appear a wide enough definition to extend to homelessness hostels where the occupants have to share living accommodation such as kitchens, though not bathrooms and lavatories.

    - Byelaws may otherwise relate to matters such as spitting in public, igniting fireworks, control of dogs and other matters relevant to public behaviour.

An allegation that a person has broken a byelaw is, of course, a criminal charge.

- Thus the local authority must be able to prove its case beyond reasonable doubt if the charge is to 'stick'. In many cases involving disputes between neighbours this will not be easy.

- It must also be remembered that mounting a criminal prosecution is a serious step to take and it is not likely that an authority would wish as a general rule to take it until all other possible ways of dealing with a problem had been exhausted.

As part of the research work carried out for the Salford and Leicester study an appeal was made via the columns of *Inside Housing* for local authorities to send copies of their housing byelaws made under the 1985 Act. Not one response was received. This lack of response, coupled with ad hoc discussions with individual senior housing officers perhaps indicates that little use is currently made of the power to make housing byelaws, although it has been said that these powers are commonly used on local authority estates (Arden, 1985). Without a properly conducted survey it is impossible therefore to learn how much use is made of the byelaws making power, and by which authorities. One explanation may be that authorities use the power only to make byelaws that relate to non–residential parts of estates and to particular activities thereon. For example the City of Coventry has byelaws for limited purposes such as prohibiting the parking of cars on the grassed common areas of estates.

Byelaws made under Housing Act powers, because they are of equal application to everyone, could be used as a means of restraining some forms of anti–social behaviour on council estates where some houses have been sold into private ownership. For example, such byelaws could control activity on the common areas of estates.

A1.3 The Use Of Covenants On Right To Buy Properties

Some local authorities stress that they use covenants on Right to Buy sales as a means of demonstrating both to the buyers and their tenant neighbours that the expectations about behaviour are the same for owners as for tenants.

> Stoke on Trent has been operating such covenants for thirteen years and has sold just under 9,000 properties this way, about 8,700 freehold and about 100 leasehold. The policy has been to stress equality of rights and duties between the tenures in respect of neighbour relationships and to this end the authority has consciously based its covenants for freehold and leasehold sales on its tenancy agreement. This, officers say, has made it easier to explain to tenants the expectations that they can have of their owner occupier neighbours and vice–versa.

A covenant is, of course, just a promise made in a sealed document, such as a freehold transfer or a long lease of a house or flat. As such it binds the original parties to it personally. But can such a promise bind the land itself? In other words, can the restrictions contained in such covenants apply, for example, to a subsequent purchaser from the original Right to Buy purchaser? The answer is 'Yes' where the covenant satisfies certain requirements that qualify it as a restrictive covenant. Three of the most important of these rules are:

- that the land of the covenantor subject to the restriction (the 'servient tenement') must have been made subject to the burden for the benefit of the land (the 'dominant tenement') of the covenantee;

- that the covenant must 'touch and concern' or relate to land as land;

- that the covenant must be restrictive and not positive.

Local authorities enjoy certain privileges with regard to Local Government covenants, see for example, section 33 of the Local Government (Miscellaneous Provisions) Act 1982 with regard to positive obligation where land is being developed. In the present context see also section 609 of the Housing Act 1985 which exempts authorities in certain circumstances from the first of the requirements outlined above. It provides that where a local housing authority has disposed of land held for housing purposes and the person to whom the disposal was made has entered into a covenant with the authority concerning the land, they may enforce the covenant not just against the original covenantor but also against those who derive title from him/her, for example purchasers from him/her, even though they do not possess any land for whose benefit the covenant was entered into. This is designed to deal with situations where an authority has imposed covenants on the sale of a house and then has parted with all their land in the area. But otherwise the rules still apply – and apply both to freehold and long leasehold dispositions. In particular the rule that restrictive covenants must 'touch and concern' land must be noted. The basic object of a restrictive covenant in a freehold disposition is to protect the land of the covenantee (ie the 'dominant tenant') and in particular its value, even though, as we have seen, in some cases local authorities may be in a privileged position where section 609 of the 1985 Act applies. With regard to leasehold covenants, there must be what is known as 'privity of estate' between the parties, but this in effect means no more than that they must be in the direct contractual relationship of lessor and lessee. However, simply because there is privity of estate between the parties does not mean of itself that all the covenants between them will be 'restrictive', and will 'run with' the land which has been leased so as to bind it in the hands of someone who has acquired it from the original lessee – that depends upon the quality of each covenant. To enjoy that status the covenants must still 'touch and concern' the land that has been leased. As a general rule, covenants which deal with lessors as lessors and lessees as lessees, as the case may be, will 'touch and concern' the land that has been leased or 'demised', but merely personal obligations which do not relate directly to the land in question will not qualify, though each case has to be determined on its own facts.

The covenants used by the City of Stoke on Trent include obligations not to use the land for the purposes of auctions, or for trade or business purposes, or as sites for posters or advertisements, or as a place for the sale of wines, spirits, beers or intoxicating liquors, or, subject to certain allowances, to use it as a place to park caravans, boats, trailers etc nor to do or permit anything to be done on the land which may be, or may become, a nuisance or annoyance to the Council, or to the owners or occupiers of adjoining or neighbouring properties. These, though they have never been tested in court, are quite standard restrictive covenants and would survive legal challenge.

Note also the following covenant from the London Borough of Wandsworth – the italics have been supplied.

The Harassment Clause of the London Borough of Wandsworth's Leasehold Covenant.

'Not to commit nor suffer to be committed in the Flat or in other areas which comprise part of the Block *or the Estate*, any acts or omissions which cause or could cause a nuisance, annoyance, inconvenience or disturbance to other owners and occupiers of other flats in the Block *or on the Estate* or which amount to racial, religious, ethnic, cultural, sexual or other form of harassment of such other owners and occupiers. 'Harassment' includes but is not limited to:

a) violence or threat of violence towards any person;

b) abusive or insulting words or behaviour;

c) damage or threats of damage to property belonging to another person including damage to any part of a person's home;

d) writing threatening, abusive or insulting graffiti;

e) any act or omission calculated to interfere with the peace or comfort of any person or to inconvenience such person.'

Of course, irrespective whether a covenant is positive or negative, or does or does not touch or concern land, or its value as the case may be, the covenant always binds the original parties, as already explained.

The types of clauses that local authorities include in covenants typically prohibit:

* the use of properties for non–residential, illegal or immoral purposes;

* creating nuisance, annoyance or inconvenience to neighbours;

* parking caravans, trailers,boats etc in front of the property without permission;

* failing to keep boundary fences and hedges in good order;

* failing to keep the garden tidy;

* interfering with common services;

* throwing refuse into inappropriate places;

* playing music, radio or TV in such a way as to cause annoyance;

* keeping animals without permission;

So far as sales of flats are concerned covenants often deal with:

* obstructing entrances, stairs, lifts, rubbish chutes, passages and fire escapes;

* unsuitable use of store areas, garages, bin stores etc;

* failing to help keep common areas clean.

A1.4 Statutory And Common Law Nuisance

Particular powers to deal with certain kinds of behaviour are to be found in the Environmental Protection Act 1990 which replaced the Control of Pollution Act 1974 and The Public Health Act 1936.

The 'Statutory Nuisance' provisions allow environmental health authorities to take action to deal with particular matters which are 'prejudicial to health or a nuisance'.

• 'Prejudicial to health' is defined, by S79(7) of the 1990 Act, to cover matters that are 'injurious, or likely to cause injury to health'.

• 'Health' is not defined by the legislation but appears to mean 'physical integrity' only (see *Coventry City Council v Cartwright*, 1975). Furthermore 'health' appears to be restricted to situations where the threat is from disease or illness or vermin or other similar infestations. The protection of mental health, at least so far as someone claims to be depressed by the presence of a nuisance, does not appear to be within the contemplation of the law here.

Matters which are nuisances at **common** law may also be **statutory** nuisances.

• A common law nuisance is something which arises on one person's premises, but proceeds to affect another's premises either by physically interfering with them or by materially affecting the use and enjoyment of them. Every nuisance at common law is an actionable civil wrong for which those injuriously affected by it have, in general, the right to sue for damages.

• Such a nuisance becomes a statutory nuisance (or so it would appear from case law decided on the predecessors of the 1990 Act), when it has relevance to health, and is capable of affecting the health of those subject to it, for example the stench from a pile of rotting manure.

• Statutory nuisances are those matters selected by Parliament as issues of such seriousness that they should be controlled by the criminal law in addition to being civil wrongs.

Statutory nuisances also differ from common law nuisances in that:

• Common law nuisances must arise *outside* the plaintiff's land and must thereafter affect that land or its use and enjoyment;

• Statutory nuisances may actually arise on the land of the person injuriously affected *provided* they are prejudicial to that person's health. For example, premises can be a statutory nuisance if their condition is so poor that they are prejudicial to the health of their occupants, even though no other person outside the premises is affected: such a situation would not amount to a nuisance at common law.

With regard to noise nuisances, however, there is an apparent anomaly. Noise may affect physical well being, but it can affect mental health and this, in the context of a prosecution, appears to give rise to a consideration of mental as well as physical health, whereas such consideration was apparently denied in *Coventry CC v Cartwright* above. The anomaly is explicable only historically. Noise is a type of nuisance likely to affect a person's senses and enjoyment of property; as such it has always been dealt with by the common law tort of nuisance. When Parliament in the nineteenth century came to deal with some nuisances as statutory nuisances, the categories of the existing law were utilised, and hence noise fell within the terms of the statute. Though there is some judicial disagreement on the matter (contrast Lord Goddard in *Morrisey v Galer*, 1955 with Lord Widgery in *Coventry CC v Cartwright*, 1975), it is thought that the noise from an animal kept on land may constitute a statutory nuisance, certainly so in the case of a dog where it is made to bark, with malicious intent on the part of its keeper.

An interesting recent example of an animal noise case was *Macclesfield DC v Ingham*, 1992 where a couple were made subject to an abatement notice in respect of six pet peacocks who, it was alleged, kept their neighbours awake at night. The couple appealed to the magistrates against the notice unsuccessfully and were given seven days in which to find new homes for the birds. It was not alleged by way of defence that the local authority had no power to issue the notice.

The Noise and Statutory Nuisance Bill 1993 will add to the list of noise nuisances noise emitted from or caused by a vehicle, machinery or equipment in a street, footway, road or square, *except* traffic noise or noise from political demonstrations. The operators of noisy vehicles/equipment will be liable for such nuisances, while provision is made for action to be taken against anticipated street noise nuisances. These new laws will, for example, apply to those who repair and test vehicles noisily in the streets outside their homes. The new legislation will also impose further controls which local authorities may operate in relation to the use of loudspeakers in streets or roads, and also with regard to audible intruder alarms.

A1.5 Possession Orders

Before the passage of the Housing Act 1980 a local authority landlord's decision to seek possession could only be challenged by the tenant in question on the basis that it was so unreasonable that no reasonable local authority could have reached it.

* The burden of proof on the tenant in such circumstances was virtually impossible to discharge (*Bristol DC v Clark*, 1975 and *Cannock Chase DC v Kelly*, 1978).

With the 1980 legislation came the notion of the secure tenancy whereby a tenant's possession could only be brought to an end at the landlord's behest by a court order.

* This court order could only be granted within defined circumstances (see now Schedule 2 of the Housing Act 1985), and in relation to the majority of the 'grounds' for possession provided for by the legislation the landlord must prove the reasonableness of making the order.

Many tenants do not realise the constraints that this puts on landlords in dealing with difficult behaviour by other tenants.

The 1985 and 1988 Act grounds are derived from similar provisions in the Rent Act 1977, itself the successor to much previous legislation. Hence a considerable body of case law exists to indicate the usefulness and applicability of the provision.

In the case of a secure tenancy, notice in compliance with section 83 of the Housing Act 1985 must have been served on the tenant (section 7 of the Housing Act 1988 in the case of assured tenancies), which generally means that twenty eight days notice must have been given to the tenant.

It must first be noted that it is not sufficient for the landlord merely to prove that the terms of the ground for possession have been satisfied. No order for possession can be made unless the court also considers it would be reasonable to make the order (see *Shrimpton v Rabbit*, 1942).

- In this context 'reasonable' means that the court must take into account the interests of both the landlord and the tenant, while the wider public interest must also be considered (see *Battlespring v Gates*, 1983).

- The court will consider the conduct of the defendant and the responsibilities that were laid on him/her as a tenant.

In *Holloway v Povey*, 1984, a case in which possession was sought on the basis that the tenant was in breach of condition for failure to tend a garden, the Court of Appeal considered possession should not be awarded because the tenant had only had legal responsibility for the garden for a part of the period in which it had been neglected.

- The rehousing of the 'victim' of the tenant against whom possession is sought may also be a factor to take into account. If that person has been rehoused the landlord will have to show that it is still reasonable to make a possession order, because, for example, the landlord has been left with a 'hard to let' home or because, even though rehoused the victim has suffered other loss as a result of the offensive conduct.

- The length of time between the final act in a pattern of offensive behaviour and the taking of action to obtain possession will also be taken into account, and any considerable period of delay or inaction will seriously weaken the claim for possession.

- Though possession may be sought under one of the various statutory grounds or for breach of a specific clause in the tenancy agreement, where a breach of the tenancy agreement does not also satisfy the requirements of one of the other grounds for possession, the court may be less inclined to make the order sought.

- It should further be noted that, in the case of secure tenancies, section 85 of the 1985 Act grants to the court extensive powers to adjourn possession proceedings, to stay or suspend the execution of any order made, or to postpone the date of possession and in so doing the court may impose such conditions on the offender as it thinks fit. If these conditions are complied with, the possession order may be discharged or rescinded. Thus, in a neighbour dispute which concerned a specific breach of a tenancy condition, the court could, inter alia, grant a suspended possession order conditional upon the offender undertaking to comply with the condition in the future.

• For the position regarding Assured Tenancies see section 9 of the 1988 Act, which provides that ' ... the court may adjourn, for such period or periods as it thinks fit, proceedings for possession of a dwelling house let on an assured tenancy.' However, it should be remembered that this discretion does not apply where possession is sought of a dwelling let on an assured shorthold tenancy once the initial fixed term of that tenancy has expired and the landlord has given the tenant two months notice that possession is to be sought. Nor does the extended discretion apply where a landlord has sought possession on the basis of a mandatory ground for awarding possession under Part 1 of Schedule 2 of the 1988 Housing Act and the Court has concluded that the landlord has made out his/her case.

The court has a wide discretion therefore to take into account a variety of factors in determining what would be reasonable, in deciding what weight to give to which factors, and in deciding the outcome.

Procedural Issues

An individual possession action will usually be listed for a date along with many other similar ones, and each will be intended for separate hearing. However, if the matter is contested and each side is legally represented, it is most unlikely the matter will be dealt with on the first day on which it is listed, and the first hearing will be a 'directions hearing' at which each side's legal representatives will be ordered to exchange details of their case within fourteen days. At least seven days must be allowed to elapse thereafter before an application for a second hearing can be made.

Further delays may occur in the hearing of an action because the defendant may request the court to use its powers to adjourn hearings, and only in cases where the defendant's conduct is most extreme will it be possible to abridge the time sequence by applying for what is known as an 'expedited hearing'.

Where the defendant is legally represented it may well be that a number of defences, both technical and substantive will be raised.

Technical defences include for instance:

- that the forms which have to be served as prerequisites to possession proceedings being commenced were in some way defective in that they did not conform to the requirements of statute and regulations, for example they may substantially depart from the form required by law, though a minor technical defect will not be enough to ground such a defence;

- that the ground for possession pleaded in the particulars of claim differs from that actually relied on in court – such a change can only be made with the court's permission;

- that insufficient particulars of the ground for possession have been given – landlords must ensure that they give defendant tenants sufficient details to know why it is that possession is being sought, a simple contention of 'nuisance to neighbours' would not be enough and the court would have no option but to strike out the claim;

- that statutory time–limits have not been complied with;

- that notices have been incorrectly served;

- that the pleadings are in some way defective;

- that a local authority landlord was improperly motivated in bringing the action – in which case the county court proceedings would have to be adjourned while judicial review was sought to consider allegations of bad faith, etc.

Substantive defences relate to matters such as:

- that the landlord has not made out the ground of possession in question,

- that it is not reasonable to order possession to be given up, or that a possession order is inappropriate and the defendant should be given a second chance to amend his/her ways by way of:

  –an adjournment of the proceedings – perhaps on the basis of some condition attaching to the defendant's conduct;

  –a suspended possession order, subject to a condition that the tenant shall refrain from the conduct complained of.

Even where a possession order is granted it *may* be suspended or stayed should the defendant make an application to the court, and even where an order has been carried into effect, it may still be possible for the defendant to seek to have the order and the warrant set aside (Luba, J, Madge, N and McConnell, J, 1989).

An Assessment of the Usefulness of Possession Actions

All the foregoing difficulties compound the problems, inherent in any litigation, of proving the case by having sufficient evidence that will stand up in court. Nevertheless possession proceedings, or the threat of possession proceedings, whether or not combined with a claim for an injunction, can deal with a wide range of nuisances such as:

- nuisances arising from alterations made to property in breach of a tenancy agreement;

- storing scrap or rubbish on premises;

- failure to keep garden and amenity land in good order;

- lighting garden bonfires contrary to the requirements of a tenancy agreement;

- keeping unauthorised pets or livestock;

- using property for illegal or immoral uses such as a drinking club;

- using residential premises for running a business contrary to the tenancy agreement;

- causing physical damage to the property of the landlord or of other tenants.

Tenancy agreements can also be drafted so as to regulate the behaviour of tenants with regard to issues as diverse as:

- sending offensive letters or making offensive phone calls;

- scrawling graffiti or other abuse on the property of the landlord or of other tenants;

- threatening behaviour towards or actual assaults on other tenants;

- control of children;

- fouling by dogs;

- noise from barking dogs;

- repairing and parking of cars.

It must be remembered that, where a breach of a tenancy agreement occurs, a landlord is not obliged to take court proceedings in respect of it (see *O'Leary v Islington LBC*, 1983) though a *local authority* landlord which stood idly by as one of its tenants committed an obvious, serious and continuing nuisance against another tenant might arguably find itself subject to judicial review on the grounds that it had acted as no reasonable authority would do, or could be subject to investigation for maladministration by the local ombudsman. Furthermore a landlord is not usually civilly liable for any nuisances committed by a tenant (see *Smith v Scott*, 1973), unless the landlord actually authorises the commission of the nuisance, (see *Pwllbach Colliery Co v Woodman*, 1915).

A1.6 Injunctions

Most neighbour disputes where an injunction is sought are dealt with on the basis of the rule in *Docherty v Allman*, 1878, ie that a landlord can seek an injunction to prevent a breach by a tenant of a tenancy condition even though the landlord has suffered no damage. An illustrative example of the application of this rule is *Hampstead and Suburban Properties v Diomedius*, 1969. Here a landlord leased a shop to a tenant and then varied the lease to allow the shop to be used as a restaurant, with a further provision that music should not be played so as to cause a nuisance or annoyance to neighbours and that if the landlord received complaints of such noise the tenant would cease playing music 'forthwith'. Complaints were received but the tenant ignored the landlord's request to cease playing the music. The landlord obtained an interlocutory injunction to prevent the nuisance, and the court stated that where a tenant is plainly and incontestably in breach of a clear tenancy condition, normally an interlocutory order should be made to restrain the tenant until the matter is finally decided. But it must be remembered that an injunction can only be used to enforce conditions which are clearly part of the tenancy agreement, and cannot be used to rewrite an agreement, ie to impose burdens on the tenant not in the original tenancy agreement.

A local authority may additionally rely on the general power to institute proceedings leading to an injunction under section 222 of the Local Government Act 1972. This enables an authority where it considers it expedient to promote or protect the interests of the inhabitants of its area, to prosecute, defend or appear in legal proceedings. Use of the section 222 power will rarely, if ever, be appropriate to deal with neighbour disputes. It is appropriate to circumstances where a large scale affectation of an area is likely and will occur unless effectively restrained by law, for example a major 'acid house' or 'rave' party where several thousand participants may descend upon an area. Similarly obtaining an injunction under section 81 (5) of the 1990 Environmental Protection Act is likely only to be appropriate where it can be shown that a statutory nuisance is likely to arise and that use of the ordinary abatement provisions of the law would not prevent the nuisance from occurring (DoE 1992c, paras. 64–68).

Legal Appendix 2
The Law In Northern Ireland

The legal position concerning nuisances and breaches of tenancy agreements in Northern Ireland is broadly similar to that in England and Wales. The Housing (NI) Order 1983, Statutory Instrument (NI) 1983/1118 provides that tenants of the Northern Ireland Housing Executive have security of tenure, and that possession may only be obtained according to Articles 27 and 28 of the order. In order to obtain possession, one of the grounds of possession mentioned in Article 29 and schedule 3 of the order has to be satisfied. In the present context the relevant grounds are 1 and 2 which relate respectively to breaches of tenancy obligation or to conduct which is a nuisance or annoyance to neighbours on the part of the tenant, or any other person living in the dwelling. The Northern Ireland Housing Executive's *Tenants' Handbook* expands upon this by providing, as general conditions of tenancies, that tenants are not 'to do or permit or suffer to be done in the dwelling or within the curtilage or neighbourhood of the dwelling any act or thing which is or may be an annoyance or nuisance to the occupiers of any neighbouring or adjoining premises.' Further conditions prohibit the parking of caravans, boats, vehicles or goods around or about dwellings in such a way that a nuisance or annoyance is caused to neighbours. For further details see Hadden and Trimble (1986).

Legal Appendix 3
The Law In Scotland

This appendix is based on the TPAS (Scotland) Publication *Neighbour Disputes : Is there an Answer?* and in particular Paul Brown's section in that entitled, 'Legal Issues and Recent Changes'.

A3.1 Possession Actions/Recovery Of Heritable Property

A3.1.1   Secure Tenancies: Grounds For Possession

Most Council tenants and some Housing Association tenants have secure tenancies. Under the Housing (Scotland) Act 1980 landlords of secure tenants can only evict them if they have grounds to do so. Landlords can apply for possession on conduct or on management grounds.

The 'conduct' grounds for possession for 'anti–social behaviour' in secure tenancies are contained in schedule 3 of the Housing (Scotland) Act 1987. They are:

Ground 1:   Rent arrears or breach of tenancy agreement;

Ground 2:   Conviction of using the house, or allowing it to be used for immoral or illegal purposes;

Ground 3:   Waste, neglect and default leading to deterioration of the condition of the house;

Ground 4:   Deterioration of the furniture due to ill treatment by the tenant etc;

Ground 5:   Absence for a continuous period of six months;

Ground 7:   Nuisance or annoyance in or in the vicinity of the property, *and* it is not reasonable for the landlord to have to make other accommodation available.

The court in relation to these grounds has *discretion to refuse* to grant an order of possession. Before granting such an order the court must be *satisfied* that it is *reasonable* to grant a decree (see *Glasgow District Council v Brown* (Sheriff court no 2, 1988).

Note, however,

Ground 8:   Nuisance or annoyance where the landlord considers it is appropriate that the tenant should be required to move to other accommodation.

This is a *management* ground which means that the landlord must establish that suitable alternative accommodation will be available when the order takes effect. But it also means that, unlike the conduct grounds, if the case is established the court has no discretion but to grant the eviction decree.

The purpose of the Act is clear that Ground 8 is intended to deal with less serious nuisance, generally a dispute between two neighbours which is not likely to be repeated if the perpetrator is moved. It is effectively a compulsory transfer, something which does not exist in England and Wales. There is some case law on 'suitable alternative accommodation' which can assist if problems arise in relation to this. It may mean that to satisfy the 'suitable alternative accommodation' rule the person being moved ends up in a better area or property.

There seems a reluctance on the part of the Councils to use Ground 8: many Councils seem committed to using Ground 7 instead. Ground 7, which, if successfully used, results in the tenant and family being homeless, is obviously more vigorously defended (Brown, 1992).

More Details of Ground 7 Nuisance or Annoyance

This is the most important ground for seeking possession for 'anti–social' behaviour. The full paragraph reads:

> 'Ground 7: The tenant of the house (or any one of joint tenants) or any person residing or lodging with him or any sub–tenant of his has been guilty of *conduct in* or *in the vicinity of the house which is a nuisance or annoyance* and *it is not reasonable in all circumstances that the landlord should be required to make other accommodation* available to him' (author's emphasis).

Ground 7 is designed to deal with serious problems. Conduct which may be regarded as a 'nuisance or annoyance' include the following:

– excessive noise or dirt;

– the use of premises for prostitution;

– blocking a water closet and allowing a sink to overflow into the premises;

– persistent abuse;

– acts of destruction;

– acts of violence or reported drunkenness;

– racial harassment.

It should be emphasised that the conduct must take place in the house or in the vicinity of the house and that tenants should not be held responsible for the acts of casual visitors to the house.

It is open to the court to refuse an order for possession if it is not satisfied that it is 'not reasonable to do so'.

In *Glasgow DC v Brown*, 1988 Sheriff Principal McLeod held that it was not reasonable in all the circumstances that the 'innocent' tenant should be evicted from the house because of the acts of the 'guilty' tenant. Here there were two cohabiting joint tenants, only one of whom was guilty of misconduct. In England and Wales the innocent could suffer along with the guilty.

In *SSHA v Lumsden*, 1984 it was held that the tenant was responsible for his wife who suffered from alcohol and drug–related problems in spite of the fact that he was in prison.

In the recent case of *Govanhill Housing Association Ltd v James O'Neil*, 1991, Sheriff Principal N McLeod held that Ground 7 applies *only* to conduct which affects neighbours rather than conduct affecting the persons who 'in the course of legitimate business happen to call at the house. The necessary ingredient is conduct that is a nuisance or annoyance to *neighbours*' (Author's emphasis).

This judgement is binding in the Sheriffdom of Glasgow and Strathkelvin but possibly might not be followed elsewhere. Nonetheless cautious landlords may consider inserting a contractual ground to deal with, for instance, threats of violence to staff (Brown, 1992, p.11).

How to choose between Ground 7 and 8

The purpose of the Act is that Ground 8 is to deal with less serious nuisance, while Ground 7 is plainly to deal with somebody who is incapable of dealing with a tenancy at all. For 'grey areas' it may be easier to threaten to transfer the offender compulsorily and solve the problem without a court hearing. Ground 7 can be used in conjunction with an offer of homeless persons accommodation on a temporary tenancy. This may be a way of controlling future behaviour for a short while, or providing support and help to a tenant who has serious problems (Brown, 1992, p.12).

A3.1.2   Assured Tenancies: Grounds For Possession

The legislation on assured tenancies is contained in the Housing (Scotland) Act 1988 (as amended). The landlords' powers to deal with nuisance and annoyance are similar to secure tenancies: although it will be noted that the complications increase substantially in the case of tenancies with a longer 'term' or 'Short Assured Tenancies'.

For assured tenancies, there is no 'management' ground specifically dealing with anti–social behaviour but under Ground 9 (schedule 5 Part II) landlords have the power to seek possession if:

'Suitable alternative accommodation is available to the tenant or will be available for him when the order for possession takes effect'.

This was not designed to be used in anti–social behaviour cases but Brown argues that there seems no reason why it might not be tried (Brown, 1992). The landlord would need to show that:

i)   the tenancy had been validly brought to an end;
ii)   the notice has been validly served;
iii) suitable alternative accommodation is available
      (as defined by the Act);
iv)   it is reasonable for the court to order possession.

This ground appears to give a landlord very substantial rights, but it is not known how the courts will approach disputed cases. Note however that it has been argued that this ground cannot be used in respect of an assured as opposed to a statutory assured tenancy. This will cause no great problems in the case of most assured tenancies which run month to month. 'Short Assured Tenancies' of 6 months or more may be more problematic (see section 18(6) (a) of the Housing (Scotland) Act 1988).

Landlords can also use Ground 15, according to which:

'The tenant or any other person residing or lodging with him in the house has been guilty of conduct in or *in the vicinity* of the house which is a nuisance or annoyance, or has been *convicted* of using the house or allowing the house to be used for immoral or illegal purposes' (author's emphasis).

This is a combination of Grounds 2 and 7 under the Secure Tenancy regime. The important difference is that, in the Secure Tenancy, the landlord under Ground 7 must show that it is reasonable 'not to provide alternative accommodation' as well as that the action is reasonable as a whole. Under the Assured Tenancy regime, landlords need only to establish (1) that the conduct has occurred and (2) that it is reasonable for the court to grant decree. They do not have to ensure there is alternative accommodation.

....

Housing Association Policy

The general policy question for Housing Associations is whether they should attempt to draft a contractual ground similar to ground 7 of the Secure Tenancy regime, requiring them to offer suitable alternative accommodation for less serious annoyance, as well as the draconian power available to them under ground 15 which simply results in a straight–forward eviction. Alternatively use of ground 9 should be considered (Brown, 1992, p.14).

....

A3.2 Use Of Interdicts

These are the equivalent of what is known in England and Wales as 'injunctions', and their use in Scotland is similar.

> 'Under the law of contract, there are standard legal remedies available against the defaulting party, and these can be used in a landlord and tenant situation. They include ... interdict (where the object is to compel compliance with the contract) ...' (Mc Allister and Guthrie, 1992 p.77).

Bibliography

Aldbourne Associates (1993, forthcoming) *Management of Neighbour Complaints in Social Housing*, Aldbourne Associates, Wiltshire.

Arden, A. (1985) *Housing Act 1985*, Sweet and Maxwell, London pp 68–32 to 68–33.

Brown, P. (1992) Legal Issues and Recent Changes, in TPAS (Scotland), *Neighbour Disputes: Is There an Answer?* TPAS, (Scotland), Edinburgh.

Conciliation Project Unit (1989) *Report to the Lord Chancellor on the Costs and Effectiveness of (Family) Conciliation in England and Wales*, Lord Chancellor's Department, London.

CRE (1987) *Living in Terror*, Commission for Racial Equality, London.

De Bono, E. (1986) *Conflicts*, Penguin, Harmondsworth

DoE (1989) *Tackling Racial Violence and Harassment in Local Authority Housing : A Guide to Good Practice for Local Authorities*, HMSO, London.

DoE (1990a) *This Common Inheritance : Britain's Environmental Strategy*, Cm 1200 HMSO, London.

DoE (1990b) *Report of the Noise Review Working Party*, HMSO, London.

DoE (1991) *This Common Inheritance : First Year Report*, Cm 1655 HMSO, London.

DoE (1992a) *This Common Inheritance : Second Year Report*, Cm 2068 HMSO, London.

DoE (1992b) *Proposed Legislative Response to Recommendations in Noise Review Report*, DoE, London.

DoE (1992c) *Control of Noisy Parties, Department of the Environment and the Home Office*, London.

Forbes, D. (1988) *Action on Racial Harassment*, Legal Action Group, London.

Grant, A. (1987) *The Management of Neighbour Disputes in Local Authority Housing*, Postgraduate Diploma Dissertation for Bristol Polytechnic.

Grubb Institute (1990) *An Evaluation of Southwark Mediation Centre*, Grubb Institute, London.

Hadden, T. B. and Trimble, W.D. (1986), *Northern Ireland Housing Law*, SLS Legal Publications (NI), Belfast.

Halsbury's Laws of England 4th edition, (1979), Butterworths, London, Vol 29.

Hawkins, K. (1984) *Environment and Enforcement*, Oxford University Press, Oxford.

Henderson, J. and Karn, V. (1987) *Race, Class and State Housing: Inequality and the Allocation of Public Housing in Britain*, Gower, Aldershot.

Housing Services Advisory Group, (1977) *Tenancy Agreements*, Department of the Environment, London.

Hughes, D. (1992) *Environmental Law*, Butterworths, London, Chapter 2.

Hutter, B. (1988) *The Reasonable Arm of the Law*, Oxford University Press, Oxford.

IEHO (1992) *Environmental Health Statistics 1990/91*, Institution of Environmental Health Officers, London.

Institute of Housing (1993) *The Housing Management Standards Manual*, IoH, Coventry.

Keenan, B. (1992) *Calming the Neighbours*, Housing, June 1992, pp. 50–51.

Laws, F.G. (1990) *Guide to the Local Government Ombudsman Service*, Longman, London.

Legal Action Group (1990) *Making the Law work against Racial Harassment*, Legal Action Group, London.

Lemos, G. (1993) *Interviewing Perpetrators of Racial Harassment: A guide for housing managers*, Lemos Associates, London.

London Borough of Camden (1988) *Racism in Camden Housing: report of the housing investigation advisory panel*, London Borough of Camden, London.

LRHF (1981) *Racial Harassment on Local Authority Housing Estates*, London Race and Housing Forum, London.

Luba, J. Madge, N. and McConnell, J. (1989) *Defending Possession Proceedings*, Legal Action Group, London.

McAllister, A. and Guthrie, T. G. (1992) *Scottish Property Law*, Butterworths, Edinburgh.

Manchester City Council (1993) *Solving Neighbour Complaints*, Manchester City Council, Manchester.

Mediation UK (1993) *Guide to Starting a Community Mediation Service*, Mediation UK, Bristol.

Mendip District Council (undated) *Tenancy Complaints*, Mendip District Council.

Menzel, K.E. (1991) *Judging the Fairness of Mediation: A Critical Framework*, Mediation Quarterly, Vol 9 no 1.

Morton, T (1991) *Dogs on the Lead – Good Practice for Dogs on Housing Estates*, Priory Estates Project, London.

National Consumer Council (1976) *Tenancy Agreements between Councils and their Tenants*, NCC, London.

National Consumer Council (1991) *Housing Complaints Procedures*, NCC, London.

NIHE (1992) *Tenants' Handbook*, Northern Ireland Housing Executive, Belfast.

OPUS (1989) *Newham, Conflict and Change Project*, Organisation for Promoting Understanding in Society, London

Simpson, B. and McCarthy, P. (1990) *Conflict in the community: Local Authorities in the middle*, Local Government Policy Making, Vol 17, No 2, September 1990, pp24–28.

Simpson, B. and McCarthy, P. (1993) *Effective Complaining in Local Government Services*, Consumer Policy Review, Jan 1993, Vol 3 no 1.

Slaikeu, K. (1989) *Designing dispute resolution systems in the health care industry*, Negotiations Journal, Vol 5(4).

Tebay, S., Cumberbatch, G. and Graham, N. (1986) *Disputes between Neighbours*, Aston University.

TPAS (Scotland) (1992) *Neighbour Disputes : Is there an Answer?*, TPAS (Scotland), Edinburgh.

Tromans, S. (1990) *The Environmental Protection Act 1990*, Sweet and Maxwell, London, pp 43–154 to 43–155.

Volpe, M.R. and Bahn, C. (1987) *Resistance to Mediation: Understanding and Handling It*, Negotiation Journal, July 1987.

Williams, D. (1967) *Keeping the Peace*, Hutchinson, London, Chapter 4.

Wilson Committee on the problem of noise (1963) *Noise: Final Report*, Cmnd 2056, HMSO, London.

Legal Cases Cited

Attorney–General v Tod–Heatley [1897] Chancery Division 560.

Battlespring v Gates (1983) 11 Housing Law Reports 6.

Bristol DC v Clark [1975] All ER 976.

Cannock Chase DC v Kelly [1978] 1 All ER 152.

Cobstone Investments Ltd v Maxim [1985] Queens Bench 140.

Coventry City Council v Cartwright [1975] 1 Weekly Law Reports 845.

Coventry City Council v Harris [1992] 4 Land Management and Environmental Law Report 168.

Docherty v Allman (1878) 3 Appeal Cases 709.

Glasgow DC v Brown (Sheriff Court No 2) (1988) SCL 679.

Govanhill HA v O'Neil (1991) Glasgow Sheriff Court, unreported, 25 September.

Hampstead and Suburban Properties Ltd v Diomedius [1968] 3 All ER 545.

Heglibiston Establishment v Heyman (1977) 26 Property and Compensation Reports 351.

Hodson v Jones (1951) 97 Solicitors Journal 236.

Holloway v Povey (1984) 15 Housing Law Reports 104.

Hughes v Holley (1986) 86 Criminal Appeal Reports 130.

Liverpool CC v Mawdesley [1992] 4 Land Management and Environmental Law Report 51.

Macclesfield DC v Ingham [1992] 4 Land Management and Environmental Law Report 19.

Morrisey v Galer [1955] 1 Weekly Law Reports 110.

O'Leary v Islington LBC (1983) 9 Housing Law Reports 81.

Pwllbach Colliery Co v Woodman [1915] Appeal Cases 634.

R v Little and Dunning, ex parte Wise (1909) 74 Justice of the Peace 7.

R v Sandbach, ex parte Williams [1935] 2 Kings Bench 192.

Shrimpton v Rabbit (1942) 131 Law Times 478.

Smith v Scott [1973] Chancery 314.

SSHA v Lumsden (1984) SLT (SHCT) 71.

Tod–Heatley v Benham (1889) 40 Chancery Division, 80

Veater v G [1981] 2, All England Reports 304.

Wyre Forest DC v Bostock (1992) 4 Land Management and Environmental Law Reports 50 and 101.

Yates v Morris [1950] 2 All England Reports 577.